C000217354

• HALSGROVE DISCOVER SERIES ➤

DAPHNE DU MAURIER'S CORNWALL

Bret Hawthorne

HALSGROVE

First published in Great Britain in 2010
Reprinted 2014

British Library Cataloguing-in-Publication Data
A CIP record for this title is available from the British Library

ISBN 978 0 85704 046 6

HALSGROVE
Halsgrove House,
Ryelands Business Park,
Bagley Road, Wellington, Somerset TA21 9PZ
Tel: 01823 653777 Fax: 01823 216796
email: sales@halsgrove.com

Part of the Halsgrove group of companies
Information on all Halsgrove titles is available at: www.halsgrove.com

Printed and bound in China by Everbest Printing Co Ltd

CONTENTS

"Until Wendy came her mother was the chief one."

J.M. Barrie, *Peter Pan*

"La mer a bercé mon coeur pour la vie"

C. Trenet, 'La Mer'

"Allegro appassianato"

Chopin, Prelude 24, 'The Storm'

"La grande question de la vie, c'est la douleur que l'on cause"

B. Constant, *Adolphe*

"But "our heart glows", and secret unrest gnaws at the root of our being… Dealing with the unconscious has become a vital question for us – a question of spiritual being or non-being."

C.G.Jung, *The Archetypes and the Collective Unconscious*

Acknowledgements

All Daphne Du Maurier quotes reproduced by kind permission of Curtis Brown Group Ltd, London on behalf of the The Estate of Daphne Du Maurier © Daphne Du Maurier (October 2010).

Page 124: *Daphne Du Maurier, A Daughter's Memoir* by Flavia Leng, Mainstream Publishing. Reproduced by kind permission.

Photos used with kind permission: Page 16: Jane Slade figurehead, Kit Browning. Page 29: Clay jetties, Cornwall Photo Image Bank. Page 51: The Jane Slade, Paul Richards (Fowey Museum). Page 68: Cornish Wrecks, Reg Watkiss Collection. Page 103: *The Cornish Guardian*, The British Library. Page 114: Castle Dor from the air, Steve Hartgroves, Historic Environment, Cornwall Council. Page 119: Map of Tywardreath, Tywardreath WI.

INTRODUCTION

Drawn up in our impressively regimented files waiting to board the ferry, the thought crosses my mind that A.L. Rowse would have wholeheartedly disapproved of the venture I am about to embark upon.

In the introduction to his *Cornwall,* he speaks out against the superficiality of books about his beloved 'Little Land' written by 'irremediably' non-Cornish authors. Will I too commit the cardinal sin of all tourists, never seeing beneath 'the surfaces of things', all the time missing the authentic spirit of the county?

*****

Looking back now, however, what Rowse hadn't taken into account is the passion that the discovery of *his* Cornwall can generate in some of us *'foreigners'*...

Fowey cast its spell over Daphne du Maurier back in 1926 and still it does not fail to enchant and delight. The river continues to glint and sparkle and exert its attraction just as it did when Kenneth Grahame described it in *The Wind in the Willows*. I defy anyone not to come away entranced by Lantic and Lantivet Bay, Polkerris or Pridmouth Cove. Where else are there views comparable to those from Hall Walk down on to Pont Pill and Polruan?
Landscapes inseparable from the novels of Daphne du Maurier.

Frenchman's Creek was read at a single sitting, lolling in a sun-lounger one hot, hazy summer afternoon. *Rebecca* was unputdownable, despite the varying degrees of anxiety that it stirred up deep in the closed-off wings of my unconscious. And then off into, what is for most readers, uncharted waters: *The Loving Spirit*, *My Cousin Rachel, The King's General, The Scapegoat* and *The House on the Strand*. Not to mention all the short stories that I had no idea she had even written! Thought-provoking books that have led my mind off in so many different and fascinating directions. Books that express, as Ted Hughes put it, 'something of the deep complexity that makes us precisely the way we are; the fleeting quality of our time in this world; the spirit of the snowflake in the water of the river'.

Above all the poetry of Cornwall, its changing landscapes, seasons and moods – all of which du Maurier captured so perfectly.

I hope you enjoy the journey as much as I have.

*****

The traffic light turns to green. Cornwall beckons.

Paignton
May 2010

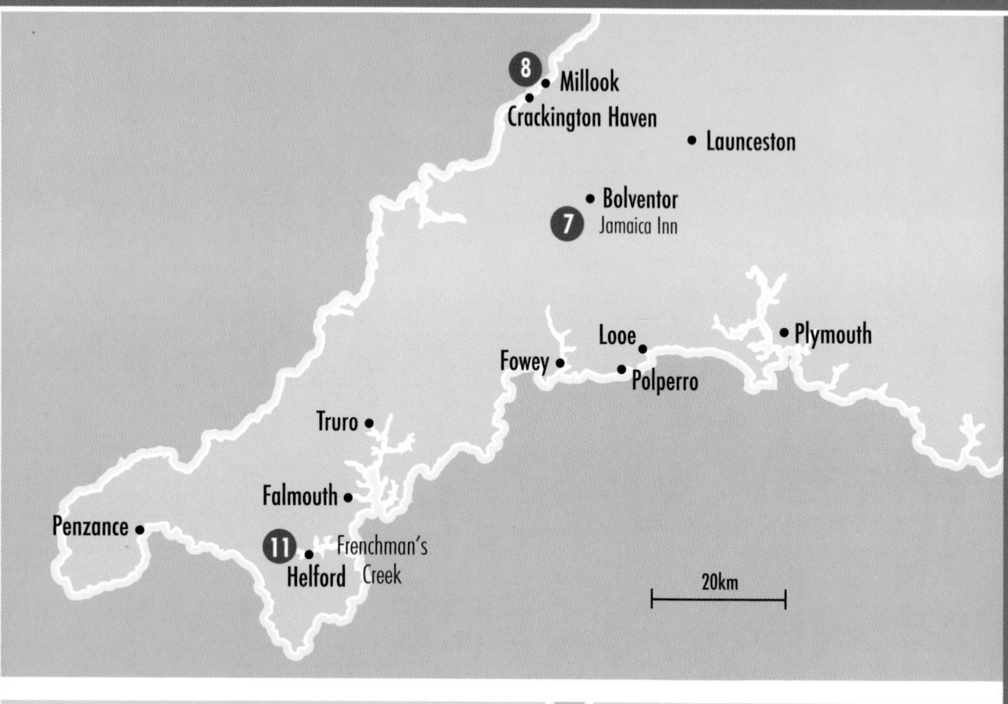

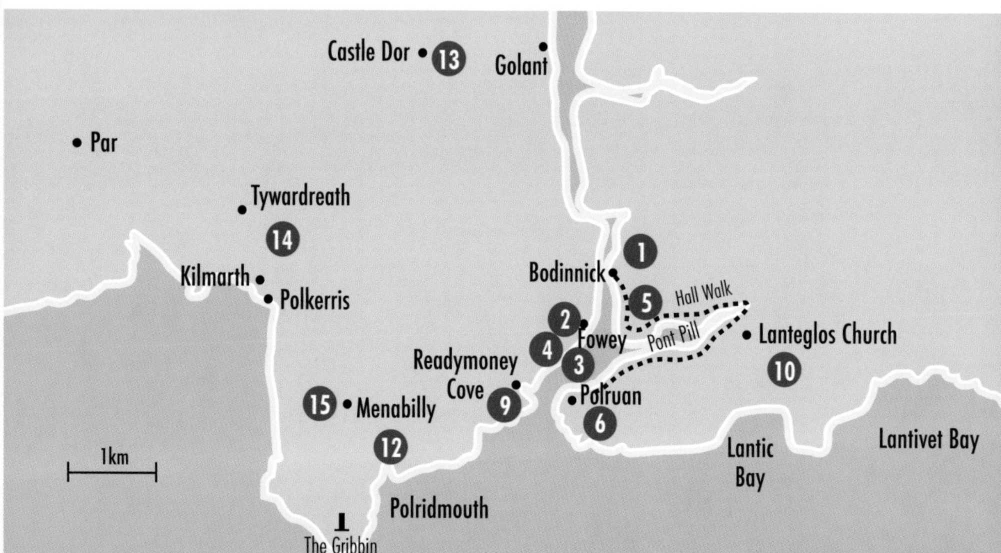

Locations

1 Bodinnick
2 Fowey – The Main Street
3 Fowey – A Boat Trip
4 Fowey – Trafalgar Square
5 Hall Walk & Pont Pill
6 Polruan
7 Bodmin Moor & Jamaica Inn
8 The North Coast
9 Fowey – Readymoney Cove
10 Lanteglos Church, Lantic & Lantivet Bay
11 The Helford River & Frenchman's Creek
12 Polridmouth
13 Castle Dor
14 Tywardreath & Kilmarth
15 Menabilly

Works and chapters in which they are referred to

The Loving Spirit 1,3,5,6,9,10,14
I'll Never Be Young Again 1,12,13
Julius 13,14
Jamaica Inn 1,7,8,9,11,14,15
Rebecca 2,3,4,5,9,11,12,13,15
Frenchman's Creek 3,9,10,11,14,15
The King's General 1,2,7,12,14,15
Rebecca 2,3,4,5,9,11,12,14,15
My Cousin Rachel 3,4,12,14,15
The Apple Tree (Monte Verita, The Birds, The Old Man) 1,4,11,12,14,15
The Scapegoat 14,15
Castle Dor 2,4,9,13,14,15
Vanishing Cornwall 6,10,13,14
The House on the Strand 13,14,15
Rule Britannia 4,14
Growing Pains 1,4,5,10,12,15
The Rebecca Notebook 14

CHAPTER 1
BODINNICK

Warships appear out of the morning mist on the Hamoaze. Five hundred years ago, downstream from here, the burgeoning town of Plymouth was growing up along the stretch of river known as Cattewater, with the Hoe and Barbican on one side, the fort of Mount Batten on the other. Cattewater was the setting in 1627 for the magnificent parade of His Majesty's men-of-war returning from the disastrous venture to La Rochelle at the outset of *The King's General*. Some 350 years later there would be similar jubilant homecoming scenes when the fleet returned from The Falklands.

Royal Navy frigate at Devonport

The freshly-arrived William of Orange, recognising the need for new warships, initiated the construction of the Royal Dockyards here at Devonport in 1690. The Hamoaze was the birthplace, but also the final resting place, of many of our most illustrious fighting craft. Turner's beloved *Temeraire* would finish her days here alongside her glorious sisters of the battles of Trafalgar and the Nile - *Formidable* and *Vanguard*. Sadly they came to inglorious ends: rusting hulks of prison ships, housing in their black tar carcases thousands of French soldiers in the most appalling conditions. Today, some of the most sophisticated war-machines on the planet are lined up alongside the quays.

The ferry chains pull us steadily towards Torpoint and the Cornish side of the Tamar.

Daphne du Maurier had, as a child, visited Cornwall twice, spending holidays at Kennack Sands and Mullion Cove. The passage by train, just upriver across Brunel's elegant bridge, marked, in her mother's words, the tremendous moment of transition from Devon into Cornwall. Daphne remarks that she felt nothing – she felt cheated as there seemed to her to be no difference between before and after.

And yet, once off the ferry, the countryside really does become more luxuriant, more vital. Ferns and fronds are everywhere - an infinite palette of shades of green. A majestic viaduct glimpsed

Red campion

Looe

through the trees marches off across a river into the distance. Waves of glistening cow-parsley, breaking over banks of pink-red campion, roll down to the roadside. Here and there, the brilliant cobalt blue of green alkanet. We turn off past a remote homestead on the edges of a shady, dripping wood and wind up and away towards Looe.

The road finally drops down towards the port, passing the station on the right. Crossing the bridge joining West to East Looe gives your first view down towards the sea. Houses and buildings line the river on both sides as it reaches its destination. Daphne had travelled here by train from Paddington with her mother and sisters on 13 September 1926. She wasn't impressed: she found the town 'narrow and claustrophobic'. So much so that the next day the family made their excuses with the owner of the small, commercial hotel, hired a car, and drove on to Bodinnick, making for Fowey.

In *The King's General*, Richard Grenville rides in the opposite direction from his home in Killigarth, near Polperro, through Looe and then follows the road, awash with bluebells in the spring, that twists up through the valley towards Liskeard. His destination: the modest farmstead of Lanrest, near the village of Trewidland. Here he would make love to the young Honor Harris while straddling the bough of an apple tree in her mother's orchard. Lanrest has long gone, destroyed by the Parliamentarians in the Civil War. Or perhaps just a fragment is left to form, unbeknownst to new owners, the wall of a cottage.

It is easy to miss the turning to Bodinnick. In which case, before you know it, you will find yourself surrounded by horses and traps waiting to whisk you off into Polperro. Once the haunt of smugglers, today it is overrun by day-trippers. Grenville's house at Killigarth has succumbed to a similar fate, ending up, rather ignominiously, as a caravan park. Killigarth, it turns out, was also home to his son Joseph's mother, a dairy-maid. When Honor protests that the child must have been conceived while he was courting her at Lanrest, he replies matter-of-factly that he hadn't ridden to see her every day! Tact was not Richard Grenville's outstanding quality.

The road continues through the village of Pelynt, passing in front of The Jubilee Inn, originally The Axe owned by Thomas Slade, father of Christopher Slade, the inspiration for the character of Thomas Coombe in *The Loving Spirit*. We are getting close. Today, with not a car in sight on the Lanteglos Highway, we are rapidly approaching our destination. Innumerable roads to the left lead off to Polruan: the countryside must be criss-crossed with lanes all leading to the same place. Signposted (and confusing) names such as Lansallos, Lanteglos and Lantivet are, for the moment, no more than vague recollections of things read, but will become more and more familiar as the months pass.

A fork to the left leads to the village of Bodinnick, while the main road continues right to the ferry (I will learn later in a Proustian moment that the two roads do in fact meet up). A

large, very visible sign announces that we are now entering 'Du Maurier Country'. I had known, of course, that I wasn't the first to come and stare at Ferryside, to look for the origins of *The Loving Spirit*, to discover the start of Daphne du Maurier's Cornish adventure. What I hadn't expected, however, was to be told in such large characters, so publicly, that I was just one of the very many to pass this way. It is with this first touch of cynicism that I wend my way down to the ferry ramp. Daphne du Maurier would have appreciated the irony that it is in great part her novels that have swelled the influx of tourists that she spoke out so passionately against.

Above left: *Looe; a 1928 postcard*

Above right: *Polperro; a postcard of 1911*

Above: *Du Maurier Country*

Left: *The Jubilee Inn, Pelynt*

Above: *The 'main street', Bodinnick*

Above right: *An old postcard showing the horse-ferry*

Below: *The food should be good!*

I make the same decision the du Mauriers had taken that day and decide to have lunch at The Ferry Inn before continuing across to Fowey. The car park is up the 'main street' on the right. Walking down towards the pub you have the classic view down to the river seen on all the postcards. There has been a ferry here for over 700 years. The old wooden painted sign shows what it used to be like when horses and carts were regular passengers. The ferrymen did not, however, limit themselves exclusively to this single public-spirited activity. In 1845, Polruan coastguards surprised the ferry trying to creep hundreds of tubs of fine brandy from the seabed off Coombe Cove. The smugglers-cum-ferrymen were forced to flee, abandoning the boat which, by this time, had been swamped by the incoming tide.

Inside the pub the walls are covered with an assorted array of mementoes, pictures and bric-a-brac devoted to the sea. The ceiling is curiously decorated with a rich and varied tapestry of multi-coloured beercloths. There is one portrait of the young Queen Elizabeth, but refreshingly, not a single trace of Daphne du Maurier. Judging by the number of Good Pub stickers on the window behind me, the food ought to be delicious. I order a crab sandwich and a beer.

And so this is where they sat that very first day – maybe at this very table. The barmaid even seems to have something of the Jane Slade about her, or is it just my imagination working overtime? The pub is empty save for two burly, tanned marine engineers in company-logoed sweat shirts, drinking cider at the bar, and three older people at a small table to my right. The small table's dog is called Ella. The man is extolling the virtues of a little, grey 1957 Ferguson D20 tractor – all in working order – bought on eBay. The woman announces in an upper class drawl that they are all off to the Azores this summer and Martin will, of course, be sailing down. Mervyn can't make it – he's doing the Transatlantic this year.

As I come to realise later, already in these first fifteen minutes, I have discovered the two very distinct faces of Fowey.

The du Mauriers had come here ostensibly looking for a holiday home. Also, we gather from Daphne and Angela's biographies, because mother and father were worried about Daphne's ever increasing visits to Paris and her slightly unorthodox relationship with her French mistress, Mlle Fernande. Fowey, they hoped, might prove to be a distraction. How right they were – Fernande's 'fascination' would start to wane from Daphne's very first moments in Bodinnick.

I stroll down to the ferry. There was a 'For Sale' sign on the gate to Ferryside, or Swiss Cottage as it was then called, when Daphne, grown restless in the pub, wandered off to explore. Never one to be put off by closed gates, private property or 'No Admittance' signs, our inveterate trespasser immediately decides to investigate. Ferryside, at that time, housed a sailmaker's and a boatyard. It had a tiered garden. The third, top floor was a chalet-style house. The ground floor was a boat-building workshop with a stream running through into the bargain. Daphne recalls that there were small boats everywhere, and a big ship guided by two tugs was about to moor a couple of cable-lengths from the house.

Ferryside – the jutting spur of rock

Ferryside from the water

Her first view of Fowey from the crest of the hill had already sent her spirits soaring. Here now was the confirmation that this was where she had been looking for. A place where she could be alone to walk, to sail, to think and, most importantly, to write. It meant, simply, freedom. And if her books sold too, then financial independence also. She crouched down, holding on to the mooring ring on the jutting spur of rock below Ferryside, and took in the river. These first sensations quickly sank deep into her unconscious. She would summon them up later on several occasions, most memorably in the opening scene of *I'll Never Be Young Again*. It was the smell of tar, rope, rusted iron and tidal water.

I wanted to picture better what Bodinnick looked like back on that day in 1926. And so to eBay in search of postcards. The nearest I can find is dated 26 June 1925. On the back a Mr Finn has written: *"Walked to Pont & had good tea. Don't think much of hotel. Plain food & cabbage. Small fox terrier met us at Fowey and came all the way with us. Enjoyed cake etc. for tea. Curious ducks at Pont with red faces."*

There is a notice on the gate of the boatyard in the postcard, tantalisingly just too small to see if it reads 'For Sale'. The cottage opposite belonged to a Miss Roberts. This is where Daphne lived while she went across to Ferryside everyday to write *The Living Spirit*. There is the sea wall where Miss Roberts' macaw would perch and squawk at passers-by. On the opposite side of the

Mr Finn's postcard, 26 June 1925

river, the grey cottages of Fowey that Gerald du Maurier, her father, would have quite happily dynamited when he looked out at them across the river on his first visit.

The gate today is open. The garden is well-tended with white walls and bright blue pots around the doorway. Writing this, I don't know if I will ever get to see the inside of Ferryside but Angela's autobiography gives a good idea. The house is built against the living rock: in many of the rooms, the cliff itself forms the wall. You can see the same effect in the family room of the Ferry Inn. The first glimpse of the long living room, with its view right down Fowey harbour and out to the sea beyond, apparently leaves visitors spellbound. Initial stage directions in the play, *September Tide*, which was set at Ferryside, make it clear that in the house you have the sensation of being right on the water's edge, with the sound of lapping water, passing ships and the crying of gulls.

*****

These first few months in Fowey were crucial for the direction the rest of Daphne's life. At last, she understood where her future lay. In addition, she met two crucially important older men who took her under their wing.

Q (Arthur Quiller-Couch, the celebrated writer and academic) was a mine of information on the history of Fowey. Right from the beginning she heard tales about the Rashleigh family and bodies immured in walls. She went with Foy, Q's daughter, to Bodmin and visited Jamaica Inn. Most important of all, she discovered Menabilly, the Rashleigh's ancestral seat.

The other is a less intellectual, but no less spiritual figure – Harry Adams, ex Royal Navy and veteran of Jutland. He helps her discover her great passion for the sea, fishing and everything to do with boats.

Her private life at this time could perhaps best be described as 'confused'. She clearly had a magnetic personality, attracting, it would seem, almost everyone she met – males, and sometimes females. Indeed, she would continue to fall back on Fernande for one or two years, seeking refuge in Paris in times of uncertainty about the course her life was taking.

Carol Reed, the film director, she found just too young and childish; she feels almost maternal love towards him.

Then there was the odd relationship with her father's brother, Geoffrey, 22 years her senior, and even more dashingly good-looking. He admitted to Gerald du Maurier that he had been in love with her for seven years, since they had first held hands on the beach during a holiday at Thurlestone. Even now when he was visiting in London, she would come downstairs in her pyjamas when all had gone to bed for a kiss and a cuddle. Geoffrey came out of it worst,

Ferryside entrance

The Family Room, in the Old Ferry Inn

becoming besotted with her, despite being married and having a wife in a nursing home. He travels to Australia and writes to her from every port along the way. But no, she writes, Geoffrey was more like a brother, albeit an incestuous brother.

Finally, of course, there was the relationship – unusual and particularly intense as noted by many – with her father. And, as she admits, kissing Geoffrey was just like kissing D(addy).[1] She recounts in her autobiography, *Growing Pains* that when she was twenty-one she wrote in her diary:

> *I'm rapidly coming to the conclusion that freedom is the only thing that matters to me at all. Also utter irresponsibility! Never to have to obey any laws or rules, only certain standards one sets for oneself. I want to revolt, as an individual, against everything that "ties". If only one could live one's life unhampered in any way*

What attracts her about Fowey is that she will be out of society and her parents' eye and free to express her individualism. More importantly, she realises that there are, and always will be, two sides to her character: "the writing me and the real me". This inner tension will fuel her creative energy and it is through literature that she will work out this inner conflict.

When she returns to Fowey in 1931 to write the fourth part of *The Loving Spirit* she has said goodbye in her mind to all that which was her life up to then. She positively embraces her new ascetic lifestyle at Miss Roberts'. It is at this moment that she first speaks of her routines, her 'routes' that would be so important to her for the rest of her life. Only in this regimented way can she dedicate herself sufficiently to her work and separate, or reconcile to some extent the two sides of her personality.

As she writes of Jennifer, the last of the Coombe family line in the novel, she is virtually writing her new persona. Jennifer is the same age as Daphne. She is scarred above all by the loss of her father, her mother hardly figuring in her recollections of childhood. She leaves London and travels to Plyn (Polruan). She has a love of boats, the *Janet Coombe*, in particular. Clairvoyantly, du Maurier predicts a marriage with a partner who shares her interest and her passion for the sea.

And, right on cue, enter Tommy 'Boy' Browning stage left. She finds him attractive ('menacing' is the word the du Mauriers would use) – and soon falls in love. He gives out orders – the first time, she admits, that she has ever experienced this. It is tempting to say that at 35, he is almost old enough to be a father figure, too.

They seem to be kindred spirits. He combines the qualities of the other two animus figures she has met in Fowey. Like Adams, he has a love of boats and the sea; like Couch he is well read and interested in literature and the arts. But he is also fascinating – an Olympic athlete and the youngest Major the army has ever had. What's more, he is a creature of routines – fanatically precise and ordered. As well as all this there is a charming boyish side to him – one thinks of the little teddy bears that he takes with him everywhere.

And, if we want to be cynical, he will be away for long periods with his work so she will not feel too much under pressure. The impression is that, interested in control as she was, she also realises that she will be the dominant partner in the relationship. Significantly, she makes no mention in the autobiography of the fact that it is *she* who asks *him* to marry her.

She also makes two other very telling statements – just as revealing for what they leave out as for what they include. Firstly Tommy Browning will, she feels, let her lead the life she intends to lead. She doesn't mention that they were wildly in love but does say that she has found someone who shared her interests, her love of boats and her love of Fowey. Secondly, she says that she has found a proper husband, not a son (Carol?) or a brother (Geoffrey?). She might also have added not a woman nor a father.

Did she realise that she needed a husband to put a damper on the emotional side of her nature if she were to achieve success as a writer? Did she feel that this would sublimate her emotions into writing and give her the solid base, the stability from which she could strike out into the literary medium? A husband, perhaps, who would accompany her to the temple of Monte Verita and wait patiently outside while she searched for her truth?

*****

There was no room at the inn so the du Mauriers continued over to Fowey. I, too, drive on to the ferry. The last car pulls up beside me, but still we do not move. A few seconds later, I realize

The Bodinnick Ferry

The Jane Slade *figurehead below du Maurier's bedroom window*

why. A pair of mallards are casually waddling up the ramp. They take their position most correctly with the other foot-passengers, and we move off.

Looking back towards Ferryside, the figurehead of the *Jane Slade* under Daphne's bedroom window comes into view. The colours are as bright and fresh as the day she was painted. This is the scene facing Christopher at the close of *The Loving Spirit* when he returns from London. Upstream, an enormous freighter is loading china clay at the first of the wharves on Pottery Bend. Looking down towards the town, a luxury yacht is motoring up against the backdrop of jumbled cottages towards her mooring. Once again the two faces of Fowey.

Mother and three daughters were all taken with Ferryside. The place would be theirs within a week. Her mother would then transform the old boat house into, to use her sister Angela's words, a 'haven of enchantment'. Daphne would become friendly with many of the seamen of the big ships, listening to their stories. She would wave as they passed and they would hoot back. Under the guidance of the old mariner, Adams, she would learn how to steer a boat in a rough sea and catch conger eels. The boy in her, who had for so long watched enviously from the wings the attentions heaped on her cousins by Jim Barrie, would finally have the adventures he had always craved.

We twist uphill past what used to be Fowey Station. Today Passage Road is leafy and sun-dappled: a wooded, walled corridor – with everywhere ferns, wild garlic and bluebells.

At the top is Four Turnings – a perfectly normal-looking crossroads. Only later would I discover the story behind it.

Below left: *The road up to Four Turnings*

Below right: *Ferryside from Caffa Mill*

CHAPTER 2

FOWEY – THE MAIN STREET

Today we leave the car in the park by the old station and walk along North Street, skirting the river, to the centre of the town. The houses are pastel-coloured: pinks, yellows and blues. The road heaves and yaws, pitches and rolls. Everything has gone just a little off-true, askew and awry. Alleys and passageways to the left funnel darkly down to the shining water beyond. This is the town described by Kenneth Grahame in *The Wind in the Willows*:

> *The little grey sea town clings along one steep side of the harbour. There through dark doorways you look down flights of stone steps, overhung by great pink tufts of valerian and ending in a patch of sparkling blue water. The little boats that lie tethered to the rings and stanchions of the old sea wall are as gaily painted as those I clambered in and out of in my own childhood; the salmon leap on the flood tide, schools of mackerel flash and play past quaysides and foreshores, and by the windows the great vessels glide, night and day, up to their moorings or forth to the open sea.*

Below: *Decorations for the Fowey Regatta*

Below left: *Passages that funnel down to the river*

The tables outside The Other Place seem a pretty good vantage point to take stock of the situation. We order a sausage, bacon and egg sandwich, so big that Betsy, our little one, literally can't get her mouth round it.

It is Regatta Week and streets and shops are festooned with bunting. Two young harbour officials sit discussing the day's plan of action. A group of teenagers walk past carrying canoes, followed by a lady wheeling a bed. Well-heeled, well-dressed children with public school accents scour the windows of surf shops for the next purchase. A Morgan complete with leather-helmeted driver edges its way

through the pedestrians. At the table next to us, a weather-beaten, deeply-tanned yachtsman in a coarse navy pullover, deck shoes and electric-blue eyes sits down to smoke a cigarette and read the *Daily Telegraph*. A couple with a dog – all three in life-jackets – pass by. Close on their heels, an entire family clad in wetsuits.

The Quay House where we shall be staying has recently been renovated and refurbished and turned into probably the classiest of the many boutique hotels available in Cornwall. Our room looks on to the water, one window looking upstream towards Bodinnick and Ferryside, the other across to Pont Pill, Polruan and the mouth of the river. The room is all creams and off-whites with out-sized designer, wicker furniture. Just the sort of decor that immediately sets your partner thinking that the whole of your own house should be redesigned in a similar fashion when you get back.

Downstairs the wow-factor continues with a spectacular dining room literally ending on the waterfront. Recent guests, we learn, have included Sir Terry Wogan and Richard and Judy. Peter, the charming Maître d' who attends to us, is German and when it comes to British celebrities he hasn't got a clue. He recounts how he once asked a group of four for credit card details when they booked in for dinner (standard practice) only to find out that he was dealing with Gloria Hunniford and guests. This is great for those of us with non-VIP status, since Peter, anxious not

Fore Street in Regatta mood

Below: *The Old Quay House Hotel*

Right: *The dining room in the Old Quay House*

to commit any further gaffes, treats everyone now with that extreme attention usually only reserved for royalty, TV talent show judges and the like.

We go out to explore. We had come down Custom House Hill on our way to the hotel. The Custom House itself is not the important-looking post office – that dates from the Georgian period. Its scallop-shaped porch however, is much older and probably belonged to a hostel which sheltered pilgrims en route to Santiago de Compostela in Galicia in the north-east of Spain to venerate the relics of James the Apostle.

For Irish pilgrims, Fowey was the terminus on the route known as the Saints' Way which ran north–south across Cornwall from Padstow. Following this itinerary meant not having to negotiate storm-swept Land's End which was the equivalent of a medieval Cape Horn for the average fourteenth-century traveller.

The scallop, it turns out, was a Galician speciality. Not only on the menus of all good bodegas, they were also said to have covered St James' body, lost in a shipwreck, when it was eventually retrieved from the sea. And so this bivalve came to be the proudly-worn emblem of those who had completed the pilgrimage. The converging grooves of the shell apparently symbolized the various routes, all meeting at the same destination, taken by the Pilgrims.

Completely by-the-by, but a marvellous coincidence as I sit here writing and sipping a glass of Sauternes – the label on the bottle actually reads, 'Château Roumieu, in the village of Barsac, was an important stopping place on the pilgrim's route to Santiago de Compostela'. Before you are tempted to think that the pilgrims undertook a journey of fine sea food washed down with fine wine, let me put you right – this was one of the most time-consuming, expensive and dangerous pilgrimages that could be undertaken at the time.

This particular peregrination really took off in the mid fourteenth century. Perhaps many of the early participants travelled racked by private guilt at having survived the terrifying plague of 1348 when so many friends and loved ones perished. Perhaps others sailed just to give thanks for being alive. On a more venal note, the trip could earn you a plenary indulgence – particularly useful if you had committed one of the more serious sins.

The vicar of Fowey took three months off to make the journey in 1332. It would have certainly made an interesting voyage, with entertaining company, too. The passenger lists feature a motley cast of characters including Henry de Champernowne and the riotous Wife of Bath.

Top: *The Post Office*

Above: *The scallop shell symbol of Compostela pilgrims*

The Old Custom House

The Noah's Ark house

No, the Custom House is the more modest, recently restored building located down towards the waterfront. The house features in *Castle Dor*, a nineteenth-century take on the legend of Tristan and Iseult. In the novel, Amyot, in love with the wife of the landlord of the Rose and Anchor, Linnet Lewarne, is about to leave on the ship, the *Devonshire* bound for the Rio Grande and is sorting out his papers. Looking out from the bay window over the river, he realises that his previous ship, *La Jolie Brise* with whose master he had had a serious falling out, is moored in the fairway. At that moment, who else but Fouguereau, the captain, should appear on the steps of the Custom House. With a neat 1-2-3 combination Amyot floors his much larger opponent.

Walking back towards the town quay, you pass on your right the Noah's Ark House dating back to the fifteenth century. It was one of the only houses left standing in the town after the French attacked in 1457. How the French came to launch a revenge attack on the town is a long story but one, I think, worth the telling.

The story starts in Tywardreath, in the hills above Par. Richard fitzTurold, later Lord of Cardinham, is 'gifted' the manor by Robert, Count of Mortain, William the Conqueror's half-brother, some twenty years after the Norman invasion. A condition of this gift was the foundation of a monastery.

Richard therefore set up a sister priory to the Benedictine Abbey of Sergius and Bacchus based in Angers in France. Over the years more and more land was donated to the priory by the noblemen of the time. Not averse as they were to a bit of murder and mayhem, this was one way for them to hedge their bets when it came to Eternal Salvation.

One of the new manors the monks acquired in this way was Fowey. The Prior, naturally, had every advantage in seeing the town prosper. He granted Fowey a charter which meant that regular markets could be held, which in turn increased the priory's revenue from tithes. It also meant the cementing of trading relations with France. The monastery needed to import provisions, furniture, wine and the like. Fowey itself had produce to sell. A typical cargo list on an outbound ship in Easter week of 1344 included horse hides, cheese, bacon, butter, feathers, cloth, and above all, tin.

When crusading fervour took hold in the twelfth century, Fowey sent ships to muster with the English and foreign convoys in Dartmouth. When war came with France, and the King's Cinque Ports did not have sufficient custom-built warships for enterprises like the siege of Calais in 1346, Fowey was called upon. The now prosperous trading town was able to provide forty-seven ships and 770 seamen, a greater number than any other port in the kingdom. A veritable merchant navy long before the term came into general usage.

The seamen of Fowey acquitted themselves with great valour during the siege. So much so that, sailing back down the channel, their tails well and truly up, they cocked an almighty snook at the Cinque Ports of Rye and Winchelsea. Their crime: refusing to salute as they passed. The offended locals put to sea to make good the insult but the Fowey men sent them packing. This fearlessness earned them the nickname of the Fowey Gallants, a name which has stuck and is still today the name of the local yacht club.

War, however, clearly made trading more problematic. The awareness of their own strength combined with a desire to increase profits and, why not, excitement after decades of humdrum trading of tin, wheat and wine meant that around this time piracy also came to be seen as a viable option.

The mariners of Fowey not only took to attacking French and Spanish vessels but also to raiding French coastal towns. This new activity got them into various, sometimes almost comic, scrapes. On one occasion, in 1346, they captured a ship, inbound from the Baltic, laden with wine, only to find the cargo was destined for the household of the formidable Black Prince, the Duke of Cornwall, who not only owned the vessel but also had jurisdiction over Fowey. Which is a bit like a bunch of Yemeni pirates kidnapping and holding to ransom a ship in the Indian Ocean only to find that it and its cargo of guns are the property of Osama Bin Laden.

But to get back to the French – inevitably there came a time when our cousins of outre-Manche had had it "jusq'au cou" with the Cornish marauders. So, in 1457 they crossed the Channel to teach them a lesson in Gallic customs. They torched most of the town – in fact the Noah's Ark house was about the only one to survive the flames. They laid siege to Place, too, the seat of the Treffry family, and it was only Elizabeth, the valiant wife of Mr Treffry, aided by a couple of cauldrons of boiling lead, who saved the day and persuaded the invaders to retreat back to the continent.

Above: *Place*

Left: *The Fowey Gallants Yacht Club*

Right: *The Greedy Monkey*

Below: *Retail therapy*

At the end of the street, I espy the Daphne du Maurier literary centre. The lure, however, of The Greedy Monkey proves too strong and I bow to the nest-making instincts of my spouse. For those of you in need of that costliest of treatments: the self-indulgent, massaging of the ego known as retail therapy, then you will find that the facilities and services offered in Fowey are of the highest order. Attractions enough, it must be said, to coax even the most recalcitrant (or is it long-suffering) of partners to make the trek to Cornwall time and again. It could just be that it was shopping that enticed Mrs Danvers into Kerrith (Kerrith is Fowey in *Rebecca*) that fateful day her Mistress died.

While Rachel rummages through the brightly-coloured merchandise, totally enamoured of this latter-day Aladdin's cave, I have my first conversation with a local about Fowey's famous residents, past and present. Robbie Williams, apparently, has a house on the Polruan side, and Dawn French often waves at kayakers from her house at the mouth of the estuary. My 'source' also tells me that she used to see Daphne du Maurier hobbling to the bank but nobody took any notice. Further back, friends used to see her out on the cliffs with her 'lady' friends – Fowey apparently enjoyed a reputation for being 'a little bohemian'.

Above: *The Old Quay House from the river*

Left: *The view down on to the river*

Purchases made, we head out into the sun

It is a beautiful afternoon, the light is glinting on the water at the end of the passageway and, as usual in Fowey, the river exerts an irresistible fascination. The du Maurier centre will just have to wait for another day.

Pont Pill seen from Fowey

CHAPTER 3
FOWEY – A BOAT TRIP

We decide to take a trip on one of the little pleasure boats that offer a 45-minute river cruise which serves as a good preface to the area and allows the first-time visitor to get their bearings. The next trip is not for 20 minutes so we have time to look around the quay.

The fish restaurant, Food for Thought, looks good with a marvellous still life worthy of Willem Kalf on display outside showing off the local marine fare. Someone next to me is saying that this is where Tony Blair ate when he visited the town, so probably a little beyond our budget. Just up the road is Nathan Outlaw's Michelin-starred restaurant.

The King of Prussia Inn (the butter market used to be held in the cool shade of its balcony) is awash with colour and doing a very passable rendition of the hanging gardens of Babylon. The square is thronged with people, and a quick survey reveals that the cap favoured by Daphne du Maurier is in vogue for the older lady even today.

A boat trip

The King of Prussia

The Bonita

Sitting now at the top of the steps we watch the kids on the quayside fishing for crabs. They still employ those hand reels of orange twine with their big, round, studded lead weights that held a fascination in my childhood. And, of course, the buckets at their sides are always proudly at the ready for the statutory inspection by onlookers.

These then are *the* steps. Seeing them now, it seems amazing that du Maurier managed to endow this common-or-garden flight with such atmosphere. For it is here that in *Frenchman's Creek* Dona St Colomb alights one stormy night as part of the plan to entice Phillip Rashleigh out to the *Merry Fortune*, his ship which, over there at the mouth to the creek, had just slipped its moorings. And it is here that minutes later Godolphin catches sight of her in the confusion and she begins her flight to Readymoney Cove.

These are the steps where, in *My Cousin Rachel*, Phillip at the height of his paranoia (or is it?) from his stakeout in a pram on the river sees his arch-enemy Ranieri skip lightly ashore to enjoy a fresh lobster and perhaps some even more enjoyable company at the Rose and Crown.

Our vessel today, the *Bonita*, describes a wide circle as she pulls into the landing stage. We cross the river and pass the strange, isolated house that is Prime Cellars. It is just opposite Fowey on the water's edge. Woods crowd right down to the back of the house. It has been in the past a boathouse, private dwelling, alehouse, even a radio station during World War Two. But most interesting of all it was rented by Sir Arthur Quiller-Couch and guests for dinner on warm

Prime Cellars

summer evenings back in the 1930s, including the likes of Kenneth Grahame, A.L. Rowse, J.M. Barrie and Daphne du Maurier. Today the large doors are thrown wide-open to let in the sunshine. But we are past in a moment, and on towards Ferryside.

A wonderful, old sailing ketch is moored just off the house. I take this as the usual state of affairs, something set up by Fowey as part of the Daphne du Maurier experience, not realising that this is but a chance encounter with the *Irene*.[2]

Our skipper's question: "Are you Daphne du Maurier fans?" meets with a weak response. I, on the other hand, am falling over myself trying to get a good shot of the house and its famous figurehead. My fellow passengers seem somewhat bemused at my antics.

Now we are approaching the jetties. With my back turned to the captain trying to get one last photo of Ferryside, I look round to see a huge vessel being loaded with china clay which is mined in the St Austell area and exported world wide for use in industry and in pharmaceuticals. I make some clever-clogs comment about ballast and am firmly put in my place. The river is beguilingly deep – 6.5 metres even on a low spring tide. This explains how these ships get here.

The most surprising thing about Fowey, I am about to discover, with its tumble of pretty cottages and winding lanes, well-groomed yachts and sparkling water, is that you can turn a bend in the river and, without any warning, rising sheer out of the water above you, soars the towering hull of a fifteen-thousand-ton, 120-metre-long Scandinavian freighter. Even more incredibly, like something out of *Gulliver's Travels*, tiny craft, totally dwarfed by the immense

The Irene

Dwarfed by the Leviathan

Pottery Corner

A Heath-Robinson looking contraption

Below & right: *The two faces of Fowey*

Leviathan, casually go about their business. To add to the spectacle, the ship is lined up against a wharf which is home to the most enormously complicated and intricate Heath-Robinson-looking contraption, bristling with a startling array of belts, cranes, ladders, observation platforms, cables and cowls. For the initiated, Jetty 4 has a Fyson fixed radial bulk conveyor with a maximum throughput of 500 metric tonnes per hour. Yes, this is the place where they load the white stuff – china clay.

Fowey, picture postcard, Fowey, industrial landscape – I try to get the two Janus-like faces into my camera viewfinder simultaneously, but it's not possible. This split personality would have been evident to Daphne du Maurier at Ferryside, for the house stands right on the cusp of Pottery Corner, as it is known. Looking downstream she would have seen a quaint old-world fishing port rivalled not even by Dartmouth in its beauty. Turning to look up-river, a scene of clanging machinery and superstructures straight out of the daily life of any one of the world's great sea-ports. And at that time, pre health, safety and environmental concerns, jetties, machines and ships, even the trees behind – everything was covered in a fine mantle of white dust. The effect would have had a touch of the surreal at night (with ships being loaded around the clock): pallid ghostly vessels and clattering conveyors illuminated by dazzling arc lights against the silent black backdrop of the surrounding woods.

However, it's obviously not a case of 'never the twain shall meet' for these great brutes got here somehow. Now that would be a good photo, for it's difficult to comprehend how ships of this size manage to negotiate the relatively narrow estuary up to this point and all the time having to dodge and side-step the myriad small vessels – ferries, kayaks, yachts and rowing boats – that continually ply the water between Fowey and Polruan. The prospect of this sight will add extra expectancy to my visits to the town in the weeks to come.

Fowey china clay jetties c.1930

*****

As the name implies, china clay, kaolin, started out in China. It was found to produce the very finest and whitest of porcelains. Sèvres porcelain from France was made from the same material (these are the plates that when they come up on Antiques Roadshow you know you should be thinking in thousands and not hundreds). Dinner sets costing small fortunes were not for everyone's pockets and when the Royal Heads of Europe started to fall so did the demand for this type of china. By then other more democratic uses had been found for the material.

The vast majority of china clay produced today goes to the Scandinavian paper industry. Because of its remarkably fine particles it can be used to beef up the body of the paper by filling in all the tiny gaps between the fibres. Its second main use is as a coating which gives the fine glossy sheen found in magazines and on the pages of the book you are reading. The list of its multifarious uses: cotton textiles (same reasons as for paper), paints, leather, cosmetics, medicines, linoleum, traffic markings, rubber, plastics, agriculture, toothpastes, washing powders, biotechnology, is endless.

A water taxi crosses the Fowey River

By 1910, production was approaching one million tons per year. In 1919, the three leading producers joined forces and took control of the up-to-then rather haphazard market and became English China Clays. However, a post war slump was already kicking in and though perhaps not wholly evident at the time, things were sliding towards the great depression of the 1930s.

This was about the time that du Maurier and her family first came to Fowey. Of course in the first months she was completely taken by the pretty, bustling little town of Fowey and the stunning countryside but she was also equally enamoured of the serious seafaring and business side of the port. Through her conger-fishing trainer, Adams, she became friends with the seamen and listened to their stories. In *Enchanted Cornwall*, she recalls how one particular ship stuck in her memory – the SS *Wearbridge*. She would wave to the skipper, Richie Bird (although apparently she found the first mate more 'menacing'), and he would respond with a blast of the ship's horn.

In *The Loving Spirit* there are several references to the industry. Janet Coombe mentions that the trade had grown up during the early part of the nineteenth century and how the young of Plyn welcomed an opportunity, however remote, to become prosperous and rich. As ever it is

Our river trip Captain

the older folk of the town, resistant to change, who voice their discontentment. Later, she pays a nod of recognition to the industry by making china clay the first cargo of the *Janet Coombe* on her maiden voyage to Newfoundland.[3]

Strangely enough, the *Rippling Wave*, built at the Ferryside boathouse in Bodinnick in 1869, was the first ship to load a cargo of china clay. Even more curiously, china clay, albeit indirectly, was going to provide Daphne with the inspiration for the most dramatic moment of the most memorable scene of her most famous novel, *Rebecca*.

The details regarding the china clay industry are the biggest effusion we will get today from our laconic Captain-stroke-guide who is clearly disinclined to regale us with other stories. We turn round disappointingly soon and have a very quiet ten minutes back to where we started. The silence of our rather dour-faced group of four middle-aged couples is punctuated solely by the click of my shutter. It is only on later trips that I will learn from the guide who lost his voice and handed out little fact sheets to read during the voyage of his fascination with the life of the little grebe and the history of the recording studios at Old Sawmills where bands such as Oasis and XTC have recorded and which featured in the BBC series *Three Men in a Boat*.

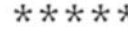

The Church of St Nicholas

The Church and Place

Someone like du Maurier who was fascinated by history must have been enthralled by Fowey – there are 103 listed buildings: 2 are grade 1 status, 7 are grade II star and 94 grade II! The two Grade Ones dominate the skyline: the Church and Place.

Walking down to the river

I will never forget the first time I came to Fowey and parked in the car park above the town. What I thought I had glimpsed through the trees as I drove in was an exotic Moorish-looking building more in keeping with the sky-line of Granada or Istanbul than a quaint Cornish fishing village. The tower with its ornate baroque embellishments is truly a surprise. So much so that walking down from the car-park I was beginning to wonder if I hadn't perhaps imagined it. Yet no, as I descend the vertiginously steep flights of steps which cascade towards the river, the tower reveals and hides itself in turns. Place – home of the Treffry family for countless generations.

Place in the mid thirteenth century was originally the headquarters for the Stewards of the Tywardreath Priory. Later the Treffrys married into the resident family and it has been their home ever since. Treffry (with the accent as in most Cornish names on the second syllable) is one of the two great family names in Fowey, the other, as we shall see presently, is Rashleigh. Place remains today a private dwelling. It was Joseph Austen, the tin magnate, who turned it into the building we see before us.

The Church, on the other hand, was started in the sixth century a little downhill from an early Christian enclosure or "Lann". The tiny community would have been surrounded by little more than a bank or ditch, with a small church and dwellings. There is place nearby which still bears the name of *Lan*gorthou. The church is dedicated to St Fimbarrus - Finn Barr – he of the golden hair - a sixth-century Irish saint who arrived in Fowey, not on his way not to Compostela but to Rome to receive consecration from the Pope. He clearly made an impression on the local Christian community for they named their church after him. He returned to Cork, becoming its first Bishop, and died there in 604.

Next, our Captain, who has regained the power of speech, points out the fifteenth century ruins of the blockhouses built to keep the French out. The iron chain which was used to bar the entrance to the river was eventually carted off to Dartmouth as a punishment for Fowey's inclination for piracy, although the odd link seems to have found its way to the Rashleigh grotto on the Menabilly estate. Some say the blockhouses were built following the 1457 French raid at Treffry's expense, though the historian Keast places them almost a century earlier.

The blockhouse on the Fowey side

An impressive handsome grey granite building rises on the next small headland on the right. Our Captain says he says he shouldn't tell us (but he does) that this is where Dawn French and Lenny Henry now live. This last morsel of information produces an unexpected flurry of excitement and hitherto unseen activity on the part of my fellow shipmates. Now it is their turn

Point Neptune

Point Neptune and Readymoney Cove

to snap away, vying for the best camera position. I don my Radio-4 hat and begin to reflect (somewhat pompously Rachel would say) on the country's declining standards and how things are just not as they were.

The position is stupendous – I hear hushed voices whispering the awe-inspiring figure of £4 million and yes, that seems about right. Location, that's what it's all about.

High on the last headland to starboard before the sea stands St Catherine's fort built, like so many of the coastal castles of Devon and Cornwall, during the reign of Henry VIII. Du Maurier would fuse in *The Loving Spirit* this spot with the castle of Plyn on the opposite headland. This is the location mentioned in *Enchanted Cornwall* when she walks one moonlit night to Castle Point and has a vision of a yet unborn son, the son being *The Loving Spirit* still in embryonic state which was fast developing in her mind.

As soon as we have passed the fort and the entrance to the estuary, the swell increases noticeably and the water becomes quite choppy. The red and white striped barber's pole of the Gribbin is keeping watch on us over towards the right.

We turn in again towards the estuary and Punches Cross, a large white cross which stands on rocks to the right of the entrance. Tradition goes that this is where Joseph of Arimathea, who was by occupation a wealthy tin merchant, made landfall, accompanied by Jesus. The cross indicates the point where those feet first walked in ancient times. It was maintained over the centuries by the priory of Tywardreath.

From what I have read it all seems perfectly plausible. But then it must be said that I am a true disciple of the living Baigent, one of the generation brought up on Thor Heyerdahl and Eric Von Daniken who steadfastly believe God really was an astronaut who, of course, used the celestial computer of Stonehenge for his landings!

Polruan

Just a little further along are the coves where du Maurier would swim naked as a young girl. Nude bathing would, by all accounts, seem to be a habit that remained with her. She never seems to have invested a vast amount in bathing wear during her lifetime. There is also the incident on the Norwegian cruise with the Jewish millionaire financier, Otto Kahn, where, to neatly side-step his advances, she dives headlong – naked – into the icy fjord, for which exploit he rewards her with a dagger. Interestingly enough it was her grandfather, George du Maurier, who, in his novel, *Trilby*, not only coined the word for the eponymous headwear, and the expression 'the Svengali effect', but was also the originator of the expression 'in the all together'.

St Catherine's Fort

And now Polruan comes into view, the principal inspiration for the town of Plyn in *The Loving Spirit*. It looks spectacular today. The village stands sparkling in the sunlight, its glinting grey slate roofs clambering up the steep hillside. As we approach, I spy some real Polruans who look menacingly back as I attempt to capture their small craft on film.

Our guide, clearly a Fowey man, fills us in on the 'rivalry' between Polruan and its more illustrious neighbour on the opposite side of the estuary. It sounds familiar: the old Kingswear–Dartmouth, Paignton–Torquay story all over again. A selection: a chain blocked the harbour but it was the Polruan people who had to wind it up between the blockhouses. Fowey is the money side, Polruan is the funny side. The best thing about Polruan is the view of Fowey. All Polruan has is a big shipyard, two pubs and a steep hill. And really in the last jibe you have in your proverbial nutshell *The Loving Spirit*. The town is dominated by the slipway of the shipyard which stamps its character on to it – the hull of the vessel standing there being a good deal higher than the cottages huddled around.

Punches Cross

Next comes Pont Pill – clearly a busy mooring place with as many masts as there were cocktail

One of du Maurier's favourite bathing coves

sticks at a child's birthday party back in my youth. Today because of the foreshortening effect of being seen head-on from the river, it seems rather insignificant, revealing nothing of the stunning aspect that it will take on when seen from Hall Walk.

And that ladies and gentleman is the end of our trip. Our Captain helps us to disembark and bids us farewell. The short voyage has been well worth it and has certainly whetted my appetite for further exploration in the following days.

Talking of which hadn't somebody recommended to me fish and chips eaten al fresco on the steps of the quay while watching the river passing by? Ever thorough in my research, I decide this information really needs checking out.

My advisors were right. Who needs Michelin stars anyway? Pan-fried fillet of cod in a crispy tempura envelope, French-style potatoes, purée of peas with a piquant tomato jus. Served! And jolly good, too.

Pont Pill

CHAPTER 4

FOWEY – TRAFALGAR SQUARE

Walking up the alley to the left of the King of Prussia you come to the Ship Inn. This was John Rashleigh's townhouse and the house he preferred. His father, Phillip, an ambitious and enterprising merchant from Barnstaple, had arrived in Fowey in 1545. His appearance on the local stage was due in great part to exciting developments in the real estate market brought about by Henry VIII.

The Ship Inn

The Dissolution of the Monasteries meant large amounts of property and land becoming available at knock-down prices. For the long-established Treffry family the manner in which this parvenu, Rasleigh, so rapidly unbalanced the local status quo must have been particularly galling. For the Rashleighs, getting a foot on the local property ladder was the best way to gentrify themselves.

That Henry's Chancellor was about to put an end to many a monastic existence was well-known, but Treffry decided to speed matters up by travelling up to London and lobbying Cromwell to relieve the Prior of his power, position and property.

Treffry, however, would not get his hands on the valuable manors such as Trenant which subsequently came on to the market. Jane Seymour's brother, the Earl of Hertford, in fact, took possession, and doesn't appear to have paid a penny, which just goes to show that being related to Henry VIII by marriage did not always have fatal consequences.

Phillip Rashleigh would eventually purchase the Manor of Trenant from the King in 1545 for £209. Later, in 1573, his son John, would buy the lands of Menabilly as the family slowly tightened its grip on the enchanting Gribbin Headland.

This was the first of a whole series of acquisitions that the Rashleighs would make in and around Fowey, their ownership of property giving them a direct influence in Parliament.

The Rose and Crown stood here

The Rashleighs and their houses were to feature heavily in Daphne du Maurier's literary production and also in her real life (this last distinction being at times somewhat blurred).

The town house appears in *The King's General* and is requisitioned and used as billets by the Parliamentarian forces. Jonathan Rashleigh complains that they cleared out his cellars when they were forced to evacuate in haste and he lost 1500 bushels of salt

When it comes to two other novels it is more difficult to pinpoint the Ship Inn as the actual place du Maurier has in mind, although she clearly draws heavily on her knowledge of the house in both cases. The reason for this is because, amazingly, another tavern used to exist between here and the church and would have stood just about where the war memorial stands now. This was the Rose and Crown, most probably the original church house inn. In 1811 the new landlord, a certain Wyatt, arrived fresh from running a public house at Plymouth Dock, was found guilty of murdering a Jew by the name of Isiah Valentine and was hanged at Bodmin. After this episode, the inn was pulled down.

So the Rose and Anchor where Linnet Lewarne first sets eyes on the onion-seller, Amyot, in *Castle Dor* and the Rose and Crown in *My Cousin Rachel*, where Signor Rainaldi lodges, are probably amalgams of the two taverns.

Just along the road is The du Maurier Literary Centre. Here you can find all her books and a plethora of postcards, pictures and mementoes. The two places that I would really like to see are Menabilly, and Kilmarth where she moved to in 1969 when the lease on Menabilly expired. The reply from behind the desk is that neither, unfortunately, is open to the public and when I ask about a view from a distance the response is just as bleak. Kilmarth is privately owned and

The du Maurier Literary Centre

Menabilly is practically invisible. "It sits in a hollow surrounded by trees. You can't even see the smoke from the chimneys." Sneaking in unannounced is also not on the cards because I am informed that the Rashleigh family do not particularly relish the du Maurier connection.

Leaving the du Maurier Literary Centre, I am somewhat perplexed as to how I am to reach the Holy Grail of my quest. I find myself opposite Bookends, an unassuming-looking bookshop which specialises in all to do with Daphne du Maurier. Stepping in, I find myself looking at the person Rick Stein had interviewed in his documentary on the writer.

Ann Wilmore, as I would come to discover over the next few months, is, together with her husband, David, the fount of all knowledge on all things regarding Daphne. Bookends is the real jewel of Fowey for du Maurier fans.

I introduce myself and my new wife and explain my predicament. Menabilly, yes, is difficult to see but the famous gates from the house are those at Point Neptune (Dawn French's house) at Readymoney Cove. Ferryside – what a coincidence, do you know Gertrude Lawrence's husband was stationed there during the war? All these little gems for the Daphne du Maurier fan pass completely over Rachel's head who stares at me as if I am half crazy. Ann tells me about *Captivated* by Piers Dudgeon, best friend of Kits, and how it really is a must-read. We talk about the meaning of the short story, *Monte Verita*, and how I think the mount symbolizes devotion to writing which left her husband to wait in vain for her at the foot of the mount. As for Margaret Forster's biography, she thinks that too much has been made of Daphne's private life and sexual inclinations, whatever they might have been. I am not so sure and propound that surely this 'inner turmoil' was the source and inspiration of so much of her work. There is no such thing as 'a happy novelist', I continue.

Bookends is on the left opposite the Literary Centre

At this point, both Rachel and Ann join forces and set on me. The result: I am made to promise that on no account must I make her sexuality a key theme of my book. I acquiesce as any newly-married man would in front of his recent spouse. But I still think there is mileage in my theory.

We walk back to the hotel past the Lugger Inn, one of the oldest in the town. As I start to climb the stairs to our room, I notice an old sign propped up against the wall. Peter tells me it was found during the renovations. It reads, 'Seamens Christian Friend Society. Home for aged and pensioned seamen'. As I lie on the bed looking out towards Polruan, I try to imagine the sailors who must have lodged here after lives spent at sea in the harshest of conditions, maybe even rescued after shipwrecks. I look around at the luxury of the room – what wouldn't they have given for this?

The Lugger Inn sign

I go to the window. From a house further along, a young woman climbs down the ladder from the balcony to the sand. She is closely followed by husband, two labradors and a child. They

The Old Man *is reenacted*

climb into a small boat beached on the shore and move off. It brings a whole new meaning to walking the dog.

Before long a family of swans arrives, and the short story *The Old Man* is playing out on the shingle in front of me. At dusk, tens of little squawky black-headed gulls skim seawards down the centre of the river towards their night-time roosts. Moments later honking geese in a V-formation arrive from seawards and then veer to the right up Pont Pill. The river, not Fore Street, is the real main road for all those who live in Fowey!

A little later, as we are sitting in the sun on the private terrace of the hotel enjoying a well-earned drink, two tugs steam past. Peter, reading my thoughts, comes to inform me that they are going to the head of the estuary to pick up a big ship.

I rush up to the room to get a better vantage point. For twenty minutes nothing happens and then there is a distant rumbling. The superstructure of a ship appears above the roof of the Food for Thought restaurant on the quay. The rumbling has now become the throbbing of engine rooms. The green bows of the Oslo-registered *Sunnanhav* come into sight. The cargo ship totally dwarfs every other craft around her. If she steams up to the wharf like this she will never be able to reverse back down river again – so how on earth do they do it? Then, in a trice, the trick is revealed. With the consummate skill and ease of movement worthy of a champion of Strictly Come Dancing our sturdy little tug pirouettes its gigantic partner on a sixpence and slowly drags her up river. For those of you who are of that bent, the vital statistics of our ballerina are truly impressive: she is 112 metres in length, weighs in at just under 9500 tons, has a draft of almost 8 metres and rises a staggering 28 metres from the waterline to her highest point.

*****

Below: *Looking towards Polruan*

Below right: *The arrival of the* Sunnanhav

Left: *Take your partner…*
Above: *Off up to the jetties*

We decide that tonight we will go out for dinner. After so many formal settings over the past few days, we feel like something a bit more relaxed. I had noticed the menu at Sam's just down the street. I phone to book. No reservations, I am told, just turn up and wait your turn. I pass this information on – my tail feathers slightly ruffled.

It's an instant hit with Rachel. What was a merchant's house in the 1380s has now something of a Parisian bistro air. Methinks mein pig-tailed host has a little too much of the charming manner with the ladies for his own good, but that is probably my Mrs de Winter side coming through. His Bohemian look is carried over into the décor of the place. The wallpaper is pink flock and we sit in green wooden booths.

The walls are covered in concert memorabilia and record sleeves. James Dean looks down on us smoulderingly from an East of Eden poster. The place is bustling, crowded and noisy. People are huddled in groups around the room waiting for tables to free up. I decide it has more of an Italian trattoria feel about it. The moules marinières arrive. Apart from being delicious, it's as if the whole population of a small mussel bed has found its way into my bowl. Life is good.

Bobby Darin's *Beyond the Sea* comes on over the speakers. The Charles Trenet original recording *La Mer* was one of Daphne's favourites – her son chose it for the opening sequence of Rick

Sam's Bistro

Sam's Bistro (interior)

Stein's documentary made shortly after her death. The CD has become one of my favourites – the actual finish to the song is quite a rousing flourish of a tribute to the sea. She clearly listened to his music a lot – incorporating his variations on a theme of *Au Clair de la Lune* into the novel, *The Parasites.*

The sea had massive significance for Daphne du Maurier. Since a very small child, even though living in London, she had grown up with the sea. Her parents took her for holidays to the seaside as a girl. She was brought up on Captain Hook, crocodiles and the islands of Never-Never Land.

The sea symbolises escape and infinite possibilities. She read as a girl *The Wreck of the Grosvenor* and *Treasure Island* and tells us in *Growing Pains* how a chair with a blanket over it could be transformed in seconds into a desert island.

When she arrived in Fowey, she sought independence but also, through Harry Adams, that experience of a boy's world which had always been denied to her – the sea, boats and fishing. It was a means of transcending the ordinariness of everyday (female) life as she knew it.

And then again, the sea also represents the unconscious where deep down your secrets lie hidden. A recurrent image in her novels is the fear of things surfacing from the depths. We find this in Honor's monologue at the beginning of *The King's General*, as a key theme in *Rebecca*, even in *Rule Britannia.*

At the trial where she was accused of plagiarising with regard to *Rebecca*, she mentions on several occasions that she had a fear of her jealousy of her husband's former lover, Jan Ricardo, coming to the surface.

She chose a house right on the river's edge; her first glimpse of her husband was as he sailed past on *Ygdrasil;* she arrived at her wedding by boat; travelled to and spent her honeymoon on the water. The sea would become an integral part of so many of her novels. Fowey might have been made for Daphne du Maurier.

CHAPTER 5

HALL WALK & PONT PILL

We climb the main street of Bodinnick. One of the most important medieval houses on the river – Hall, the home of the Mohun family – originally stood near here. In the sixteenth century they laid out the ornamental promenade high up above the river, sanded for bowling and bordered by summerhouses, which would come to be known as 'Hall Walk'.

An inauspicious start along the back of gardens is soon forgotten when you arrive at the granite war memorial. The view down to the town and out towards the sea is breathtaking. No wonder du Maurier, remembering in *Growing Pains* her first walk along the path with her trusty Bingo, quotes Rimbaud's *Bateau Ivre* in her heady expression of the immense feeling of release she experienced. Wonder, glory, content and peace are the words used by a woman who feels she has finally found her destiny.

The Old Quay House from Hall Walk

During the Civil war, the Parliamentarians were hemmed in on the stretch of land between Fowey and Par. The Royalists had used Hall Walk to reach Polruan to secure the commanding position of the Block House for their guns and so control the traffic in and out of the port. The King came to visit and review the troops. A plaque written by Foy Quiller-Couch inside one of the shelters near the monument to her father records the place where on 17 August 1644 a fisherman was killed by a musket fired from Fowey on the exact spot the King had been standing moments before.

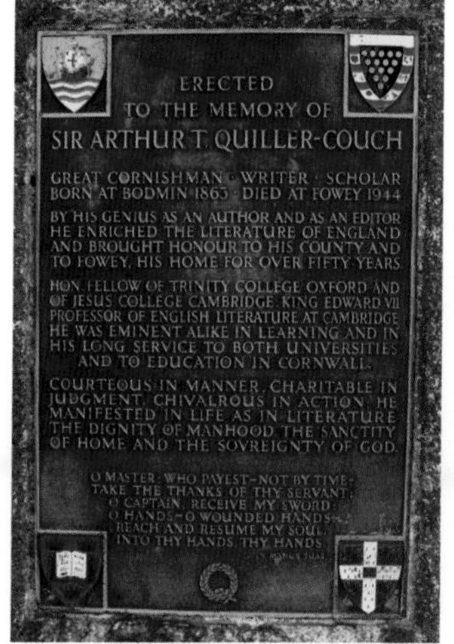

The inscription on Q's memorial

Q's memorial overlooking his beloved Fowey is a massive granite monolith. It is from this precise point that Daphne du Maurier would have got her very first glimpse of the *Jane*

Above: *The view over Fowey from the War Memorial.* Below left: *The same view in 1905.* Below right: *The same view 20 years later.*

Slade lying slightly on her side, left to rot in the mud near the entrance to the Pill on the opposite bank.

A fellow walker, noticing my camera, tells me to follow her and she will show me where I can get the best shot of the Pill. Hilary lives in St Austell but is originally from Fowey. She tells me how the Pill has been dredged in recent years since one of the main attractions for second home owners is the mooring place which comes with the house.

The sun is rising higher in the sky creating a sort of haze. I hear the distant sound of bells calling across the creek moments before the tower of Lanteglos church breaks the skyline. "My relatives are all buried in the churchyard there," Hilary tells me. Many of the Slade family who inspired the novel *The Loving Spirit* are buried there too amongst the ivy and the primroses. Many also had their weddings in the church. And it was in the same church that the young Daphne du Maurier married Major Browning on 19th July 1932.

Looking over towards Polruan

The tower of Lanteglos church breaks the skyline

Hilary's recommended view of the Pill

Looking back along the path towards the Gribbin

The path rises, falls and twists along the crest of the pill. Carew writing around 1585 uses some marvellous turns of phrase to describe this enchanting walk banked with sweet-scented flowers.

> *It does not lead wearisomely forthright but yieldeth varied and yet not over-busy turnings, as the grounds opportunity affordeth, which advantage increases the prospect.*" [And what a prospect it is]: "*the vast ocean sparkled with ships that continually this way trade, forth and back, to most quarters of the world. Nearer home they take view of all sized cocks, barges and fisher boats hovering on the coast.*

The sun is becoming hot – it is probably the best day of summer so far as we draw to the end of yet another dismal, drizzling, and depressing season. In the distance is the Gribbin daymark and somewhere in the trees hidden to the right, Menabilly. And everywhere on the glinting water there are boats, boats and more boats.

The path opens out into clearings where the buzz of insects fills the air. There are butterflies and birdsong. A cow somewhere behind a hedge is lowing. Voices drift up to us from the creek below and the path starts to descend to the little settlement of Pont.

The now redundant quay once fulfilled an important role, serving the scattered farms and hamlets in the area. Here barges and schooners (maybe even the *Jane Slade*) would have

Right: *Pont Pill, as it was*

Below: *Notice on the quay at Pont Pill*

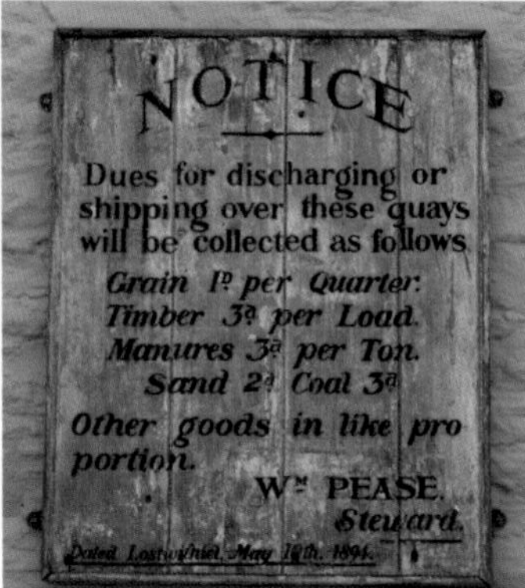

Looking back towards Fowey from the Polruan side of the Pill

unloaded coal, manure, timber and also limestone for the nearby lime kiln before taking on board the fresh produce from the local farms. A noticeboard dated 1894 lists the unloading tariffs levied at the quay – it cost you 3d, for example, for every ton of dung discharged.

The other walkers move off and a marvellous hush descends on the proceedings. The air is warm and still. Not a ripple breaks the mirror-like surface of the pool. Water and leaves slip silently under the bridge as the tide ebbs into the creek. Downstream, a swan half unfurls its wings in the manner of a sail and glides effortlessly away.

This timeless place is where Daphne and her husband-to-be would have alighted on their wedding day, having left Ferryside at 8 o'clock in the morning to catch the rising tide. She was dressed in the simple light blue serge outfit that her mother had ironed the night before. They would have then made their way up the bower-like path that leads through the woods at the head of the creek towards Lanteglos church.

Wooden steps lead up into the woods on the other side of the Pill. Halfway along the bank a road leads down to Pengegon. Here in the 1930s, the young writer Leo Walmsley set up house

Swans on the Mill Pond

The chimneys of Polruan

(he was avoiding creditors up-country) with his young wife in a dilapidated ex-army hut. His book *Love in the Sun* sets out to be a plot-less account of the life of a writer writing his first novel. He certainly succeeds in this intention and their life must have been idyllic, but the book as a whole, despite du Maurier's enthusiastic introduction, falls rather flat – it's *The Swiss Family Robinson* without the adventure.

Further along the creek again was the old isolation hospital of the port where visiting seamen suffering from infectious diseases were sent in quarantine to recuperate. In *Growing Pains* du Maurier recounts how on a furtive trespassing expedition, she peered into the windows of the hut where so many seamen had died at the end of the war with Spanish flu (she is embellishing somewhat – it saw little use). It is here that she first took real notice of the abandoned hulk of the *Jane Slade*. Here that she started to imagine the people who had sailed in her, the voyages she had made, and the story that could be told. Just there down through the trees would have been the place where the *Jane Slade* lay. This is where she clambered over the old schooner, rummaging through dusty boxes of long-forgotten letters. This quiet, secluded spot on the banks of Pont Pill was the real starting point of her literary adventure.

She would be drawn back to this mystical spot many times in her later works. The Frenchman and his band in *Frenchman's Creek* would come stealthily down this creek in their attack on Fowey. In *Rebecca*, this is the place where the *Je Reviens*, craned on to the lighter, is taken, safe from prying eyes, to lie on the mud at low tide. The water will drain out of her and the hull will be examined. With the body of Rebecca lying on the floor of the cabin.

The path eventually emerges from the woods; roofs and chimneys come into view and we find ourselves in the network of narrow alleys at the back of Polruan.

CHAPTER 6
POLRUAN

We turn left just before The Haven and take the path down to the ferry. On a ledge below, an artist is engrossed in a watercolour of the picturesque village on the opposite side of the river. For those on the du Maurier pilgrimage, a visit to Polruan would have to be the second station of the cross. There and just around the corner in Pont Pill is where it all started.

We climb aboard the little vessel. There are a few tourists, but mainly Polruans, returning from an expedition to Fowey. In minutes we are approaching the cove where the village stands. As is often the case in Cornwall, I have read at least three possible explanations as to the meaning of the name. First, Pol (pool) and ruan (river) – the pool by the river. Another that it was originally Porthruan, that is to say, the cove of (St) Ruan, an early Irish saint. But the one that attracts me most is the theory that it means 'the Roman port'. This ties in beautifully with what we know of the tin trade here with the ancient world, the Punches Cross legend and recent archaeological discoveries at Readymoney Cove.

The Haven from the river

The Polruan ferry

Polruan – the shipyard

Whatever the etymology, historians are agreed that Polruan as a fishing community predates Fowey. As we approach, you can see how the little harbour, nestling as it does in a crook of the arm of the river, would have been sheltered from the worst of the winds and also tucked away out of sight of enemy vessels passing up the English Channel.

Fishing – and by that I mean the ubiquitous Cornish pilchard – was the mainstay of the village for many centuries. The industry continued to flourish through the nineteenth century while that of Fowey was already in decline. The old guidebooks abound in references to the malodorous nature of the area. In 1898, one described "one of those half-foreign looking ports, dear to the artistic eye rather than the sensitive nose." In 1794, a traveller wrote that: "long before we landed at Fowey, our olfactory nerves were assailed by the effluvia of salted pilchards."

There was a definite season for the fishing – there is a passage in *Vanishing Cornwall* where du Maurier recalls how as a child she was called out to witness the arrival of the vast shoals of fish. Wilkie Collins does some mathematics to show the scale of the numbers involved. At the small fishing cove of Trereen, in August 1850, 600 hogsheads were landed in a week. With each barrel containing around 2400 fish, that means that in just seven days a staggering one and a half million pilchards were caught by this one community.

Polruan beach

The quay at Polruan

You can see now that the village is basically a steep road with cottages on either side running straight down to the port. What dominates the scene, as it has continued to dominate the village both literally and metaphorically over the last 150 years, is the shipyard right in the middle of the waterfront. The ship pulled up on the slipway is taller than the surrounding cottages. Next to it is a rather sorry-looking little scrap of sand where, nevertheless, children are happily splashing about in the water. This is a day at the seaside in Polruan.

Du Maurier's first contact with the community had been her fishing and sailing mentor, Harry Adams. He had married the very pretty (judging from the photos) Dora Slade who was the grand-daughter of Jane and Christopher Slade. Dora could still remember the ship, the *Jane Slade* in her sailing days. More importantly, Harry introduced her to another grandchild, Ernie, who was running the yard at that time and who, crucially, was able to procure for her the Slade family letters and the boatyard records.

She soon got down to the meticulous historical research which over the years was to become one of her trademarks. She was captivated by this tale of authentic Cornish folk. She talks in *Vanishing Cornwall* about this hardy race of seamen with energy, courage and a zest for exploration who have inherited from their ancestors a legacy of tough endurance and the ability to withstand hardship, hunger and poverty. She felt, at last, that she was getting to grips with the real world after the theatrical make-believe of London.

We disembark and pass the Lugger Inn. Polruan's other pub, the Russell Inn, belonged to Jane Salt's family. I spotted it as we tied up at the jetty – its name is written in big white letters on the slate roof.

So this is the boatyard where the *Jane Slade/Janet Coombe* was launched. Janet expired beatifically as the boat splashed down into the water, the vessel receiving her spirit as it did so. Here du Maurier changed history as, in reality, it was Christopher

Below left: *The Lugger Inn*
Below right: *The Russell Inn*

To the hills!

Slade who passed away first, leaving his wife to carry on the running of the boatyard under the name of Jane Slade & Sons. He died in February 1870 and may just have seen work beginning on the ship which was launched on 25 June in the same year. Jane's son, Thomas, was her first master. Thomas was his mother's favourite and the inspiration for perhaps the most memorable character of the novel, Joseph Coombe.

I climb the hill intending to search for Ivy House, the house where the fictional Janet and Thomas live in the novel. But I get side-tracked and branch out to the left to look down on the shipyard from above. The cottages along the lane have the split doors and long staircase windows typical of old Cornwall. A flaking sign at the end of the road reads simply, "To the hills".

Daphne du Maurier did not forget her 'debt' to the yard. She put business their way, having a fishing lugger, the *Marie Louise*, built there in 1928. The yard, however, was long past the halcyon days when it had turned out the *Jane Slade* and some of the biggest ships to be built on the river – the 243 ton *Koh-i-Noor* in 1876 and the *E.S. Hocken* of 296 tons in 1879. As the years passed, the yard steadily started to lose out as iron ships took over. They tried to adapt, downsized and turned to smaller commissions for yachts and ship repairs. But what finally scuttled the company was when, in 1919, they overstretched themselves by rashly taking on the repairs of the huge *A.B. Sherman*, a captured war prize. The work needed was extensive – a new jetty was constructed in Pont Pill for the process and even more manpower was taken on. Two long years later the work was finally finished at a cost of £6,535 – a tremendous figure in those days. Unfortunately, the company who owned the ship went bankrupt and the debt was never paid.

The Jane Slade

Despite this enormous setback the business still just managed to cling on. When the sailing vessels came to the end of their useful life, they were simply abandoned in Pont Pill – it was simply too costly to break them up. One of these was the *Jane Slade*. She made her final voyage on 7 July 1924 from London, calling in at Cardiff, Kirkaldy, Queensferry and Hull before arriving in Fowey on 6 November. This means she had been there only a few years when du Maurier first set eyes on her. She was presumably still reasonably intact, and complete, as we know, with figurehead.

When the business was eventually sold up in 1943, it was to a certain Mrs D. Browning. By buying it, she enabled Ernie Slade, already in poor health, to carry on living in his home above the yard.

I walk up to Ivy House, which is now Holly House. It is about the only house on the street with a large front garden, as mentioned in the novel. There is the big bedroom above the porch where Thomas and Janet slept on their wedding night.

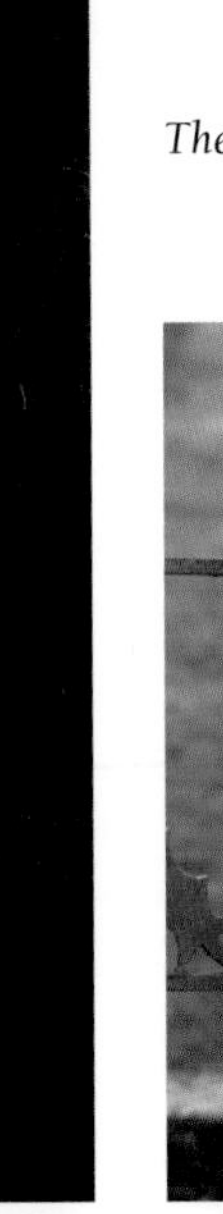

The Jane Slade *left to rot in the Pill*

Holly House and gate

On the headland above Polruan

We climb up to the headland, which, combined imaginatively with St Catherine's on the opposite bank, was the location for so many of the key scenes of the book. It is here that the novel opens with the wonderfully evocative description of Plyn:

> *Although the sun was already high in the heavens, the little town was still wrapped in an early morning mist. It clung to Plyn like a thin pale blanket, lending to the place a faint whisper of unreality as if the whole had been blessed by the touch of ghostly fingers. The tide was ebbing, the quiet waters escaped silently from the harbour and became one with the sea, unruffled and undisturbed. No straggling cloud, no hollow wind broke the calm beauty of the still white sky. For one instant a gull hovered in the air, stretched his wide wings to the sun, then cried suddenly and dived, losing itself in the mist below.*

The feelings expressed are the same du Maurier must have experienced when she first arrived in Fowey. She was on the brink of a new life, a new start, about to plunge into the world of the professional writer. Today, a kite is flying as if to symbolise the freedom of this place. The ever-present Gribbin daymark is visible off in the distance.

We walk back down to the harbour. House prices are, as I expected, exorbitant, far beyond the reach of local inhabitants. As in Dartmouth and Fowey 'affordable' housing is being built – up, back and behind the town – for the local population. The centre of old Polruan is taken up with the letting business.

This situation dates back to the 60s – Tom Hunkin being one of the first 'victims'. After the death of her husband, Daphne du Maurier sold the boatyard. The new owners sold Hunkin's cottage and took him to court to get him evicted. The judge upheld the order, ruling that the tenancy agreement was invalid and that he lived there only at the 'whim' of the author. Du Maurier, returning from a trip abroad, was furious when she learnt what had happened and wrote to the *Western Morning News* to protest. Unfortunately for Tom it was too late, the eviction order stood and he had to leave his home.

Such is life. Polruan provided the manpower and the graft for the area. It bore the brunt of the fluctuation of the labour demands during the cycles of boom and depression – first of shipbuilding and subsequently of the china clay industry. The railway never arrived here and anyway there would have been nowhere for the tourist industry to expand to. Polruans watched as Fowey developed and prospered, and as the Fowey people ate the fish they caught, built big houses on the back of the work of their men and spent their money in their new shops.

Back down on the quay, Polruan's youth sit dejectedly in a shelter near the ferry – skateboards, baseball caps, chains and unlaced trainers.

Polruan beyond the rhododendrons

Tickets please!

Yet tenacity and authenticity are precious gifts. And, more often than not, they have nothing to do with wealth and riches, grand houses and all the trappings that go with them. Du Maurier appreciated that. Polruan will always have *The Loving Spirit* – there would be no novel written about Fowey.

We climb down onto the bobbing little launch for the return journey (the Slades, by the way, built the first ever motor ferry here in 1911). As the group of girls opposite discuss their shopping outing across the water and my neighbour negotiates with the skipper the tariff for his dog, we bid Polruan goodbye.

Leaving Polruan

CHAPTER 7

BODMIN MOOR & JAMAICA INN

I leave Paignton on a drizzly wet May morning. I have a memory of a golden gorse-lined corridor as I drive over a deserted Dartmoor. The sun breaks through and in the distance is the bright ribbon of the Tamar, the bridge and the thousands of tiny boxes that make up the suburbs of modern Plymouth.

The road twists and winds as it climbs out of the old stannary town of Tavistock and at Milton Abbot I stop by a church and look at the uplands of Bodmin Moor silhouetted on the skyline. Now the roads drops and turns gently as trees close in overhead. A dappled rhododendron-lined bower leads down to a narrow bridge over the river. This is my favourite way into Cornwall.

I stop at Launceston for a pasty. Stepping out of the shop, I find myself in front of the White Hart Hotel in the square where Jem Merlyn in *Jamaica Inn* had tried to sell his painted, purloined pony. Next, a quick visit to the castle. In *The King's General*, Richard Grenville is detained here during the Civil War. Launceston has the dubious privilege of being the place that Honor Harris hated most in the world.

Above: *Crossing the Tamar at Greystone Bridge*

Far left: *The church at Milton Abbot, Bodmin Moor in the distance*

Left: *The White Hart Hotel, Launceston*

The Castle, Launceston

Then it is a flying visit to Altarnun, home of the unnerving albino vicar who Mary Yellan mistakenly trusts for so much of *Jamaica Inn*. The houses are pretty and a stream runs through the centre of village. The vicarage is half-hidden by a screen of exotic shrubs. Today they are hanging the bunting for the Parish fête. From here to Jamaica Inn it is only three minutes by car along the A30.

The dual carriageway is a scar across the landscape but it has kept the moor intact – it is far more difficult to stop and get out than it is on Dartmoor. The road follows the route of an ancient, some even say Roman, ridgeway. Although in 1260 it was already being referred to as the Royal Cornish Way, it had become little more than a muddy cart-track by the 1700s. As a result, mid-century, posts were set up at quarter-mile intervals to mark the route and the Bodmin Turnpike Trust was formed to oversee improvements. Jamaica Inn came into being in 1750.

I come up over the brow of a hill, there is a valley and Jamaica Inn stands on the other side. I turn off, avoiding a crow picking at the carcass of a dead rabbit in the middle of the road.

The Church and the Vicarage (right), Altarnun

Jamaica Inn, an old postcard

Jamaica Inn today

Mary Yellan's room above the porch

The old sign (top) and the new sign (above).

Admittedly it is early, but the place still seems strangely quiet. The dark slate of the cladding heightens this feeling. There is a huge rusting anchor in the car park. Mary Yellan's room was the one above the front porch – maybe I will be allowed to see it. A man eyes me suspiciously from a downstairs window. I find a door that is open but the reception is deserted. I go through to the bar and call 'Hello' a couple of times but nobody appears. I decide to leave.

A couple of weeks later I make a more successful visit. We leave the car under a skull and cross bones flag and make our way towards the gift shop. There is a good selection of du Maurier books and DVDs. There is also a vast array of the most disparate souvenirs: jigsaws, thimbles, lighters, tea towels, cuddly toys and key rings. Yet something is wrong: the theme of pirates seems to have taken over from that of smugglers – a tribute perhaps to the selling-power of Johnny Depp. My daughter buys a 2-foot long pen with Jamaica Inn written on it, and is happy.

The gift shop houses the original sign depicting a grim-looking character with a stage coach in the background. On the present sign hanging outside, our gentleman has mysteriously acquired a parrot, strongly reminiscent of Long John Silver.

Du Maurier invests the description of the sign with a sinister sense of foreboding,

> *A noise came from the far end of the yard, a curious groaning sound like an animal in pain. It was too dark to see clearly, but she could make out a dark shape swinging gently to and fro. For one nightmare of a moment, her imagination on fire with the tales Joss Merlyn had told her, she thought it was a gibbet, and a dead man hanging. And then she realised it was the signboard of the inn, that somehow or other, through neglect, had become insecure upon its nails and now swung backwards, forwards, with the slightest breeze.*

We wander through the vast self service restaurant. People queuing push their trays along the aluminium runway that leads to the check-out. I remember A.L. Rowse's quote – "Nowadays the inn is only haunted by coaches". Here I am quite sure they could feed nine coachloads arriving simultaneously. I find myself unwittingly standing on a brass plaque in the floor which announces: "This is where Joss Merlyn was murdered"

I decide to visit the Daphne du Maurier museum. A disembodied voice informs me this is Mary Yellan leaving Helford for the Inn. I press on to find the du Maurier memorabilia. There is the famous writing desk, caged in another mullion-window-fronted booth. Du Maurier herself was embarrassed when, driving past in later years, she saw what was happening to the place – she felt herself to blame.

It hasn't always been like this. Originally there were just four rooms downstairs and five up. By 1778, however, it was already extended due to the increase in traffic. It was at this time that the

Inn was hung with slate. This feature, which does so much to give the place its bleak appearance, not only kept out the driving rain but also conveniently disguised the join of the extension.

London Inn at Five Lanes and The White Hart at Bodmin were coach stages. Jamaica Inn was a posting house. Regular stops were necessary – in 1805, the Falmouth to London stage-coach took 41 hours! A three-foot long horn was blown to warn of arrival and sounded all the time in fog. Presumably, there were also postillions who could be struck by lightning. Redding, in 1842, writes that the Inn offered "coarse, but clean accommodation". In 1880, under Methodist pressure it became The Jamaica Inn Temperance Hotel.

In November 1930, Daphne du Maurier came here on a riding expedition with Foy, Quiller-Couch's daughter. The first sight of the Inn gripped her imagination almost as much as Menabilly. The two of them rode off to call on an acquaintance living at Trebartha Hall near North Hill. As can often happen on the moor, the weather changed suddenly and rain closed in. They seek refuge in an abandoned, ruined cottage above the waters of Withey Brook. After sheltering from the cloudburst for over an hour, and with darkness falling, they start to make their way back. They stumble upon a disused railway track which has their mounts slithering and sliding. Du Maurier comments that a railroad in mid-moor seemed a complete impossibility! The horses finally led them back to safety. As for the trolley track, she says that a diligent search has since revealed no trace of it.

A year later she returns. She reads *Treasure Island* over a roaring fire. She visits the village church at Altarnun and in the evening a 'little parson' calls upon her. And so *Jamaica Inn* is born.

The River Fowey near Bolventor

*****

Du Maurier's fourth novel lurches out of the starting blocks in true Gothic-thriller style, creaking and swaying round rain-swept bends on a journey strongly reminiscent of Jonathan Harker's classic arrival in Transylvania. It then careers, at the start of chapter 2, headlong into the formidable Uncle Joss. His description – perhaps it is the fact that within a paragraph he is compared to four different members of the animal kingdom – brings to mind, more than anything else, the hirsute perpetrator of the *Murders in the Rue Morgue*.

In this way is Mary Yellan catapulted from the quiet waters of Helford into the dark turmoil of Bodmin Moor. The influence of *Treasure Island* is clearly discernible, though with its youthful exuberance the novel lacks Stevenson's terseness and economy of style.

I decide to try to find the cottage under Kilmar Tor that Daphne and Foy had taken shelter in that stormy afternoon back in 1930. She would site Jem Merlyn's somewhat neglected cottage in the same location.

The deserted cottage below Kilmar Tor

Above: *The Cheesewring*

Right: *Kilmar Tor*

Dozmary Pool

The road south from the Inn runs alongside the Fowey river at the beginnings of its journey. The beech-lined, clear-flowing stream is a delight. A mile or so further down the road we take a dog-leg back towards Kilmar. We arrive at a gate – the entrance to a farm – where the road ends. I get out to survey the scene. And there on the other side of the Withy brook, below Kilmar Tor, is a solitary cottage…

And the impossible railway track? A quick investigation reveals we are near the ex-Caradon copper mines. A railway line was completed in 1846 to service the mines and also the new granite quarries at the Cheesewring. By 1858, the company had constructed an extension line to Bearah and Kilmar Tors. Although the granite industry continued to thrive, the copper mines had been depleted by the 1890s and keeping the line open was uneconomical. Much of the track was lifted and shipped out to the Western Front in the First World War.

*****

Seeing as we are so close, we decide to pay a visit to Dozmary Pool, subject of one of the more orthodox canvases painted by the Vicar of Altarnun.

Brown Willy (right) and Roughtor (left) from Dozmary Pool

I had read so much about this 'bottomless' pool, about its mystery and its changing moods. About how, impossibly, it ebbs and flows in tidal fashion and has a whirlpool in its midst. Here, after Arthur is slain by Mordred at Slaughterbridge, Bedivere hurls Excalibur into the depths only for the sword to be caught by a thrice-waving hand. Dozmary – where the evil John Tregeagle, steward to Lord Robartes of Lanhydrock, hated by all his tenants, was condemned for all eternity to empty the pool with a holed-limpet shell, whilst checking accounts which were always a farthing out.

The disappointment was immense. There can be fewer more insignificant, uninspiring stretches of water. And totally non-photogenic, to boot. I did discover a couple of interesting facts about the pool, however. The first that in the weeks before D-Day there were thousands of nervous American GIs camped out here awaiting their fateful call to duty. Their General, a certain George Patten, lodged at Jamaica Inn.

The second that Dozmary was once home to Captain Henderson's English Natural Ice Company. The business took advantage of the significantly colder winters of the late nineteenth and early twentieth century. A large wooden store was erected capable of holding the 600 tons of ice which was cut from the surface of the pool. It was covered with peat and left till the ice was

The path up to Roughtor

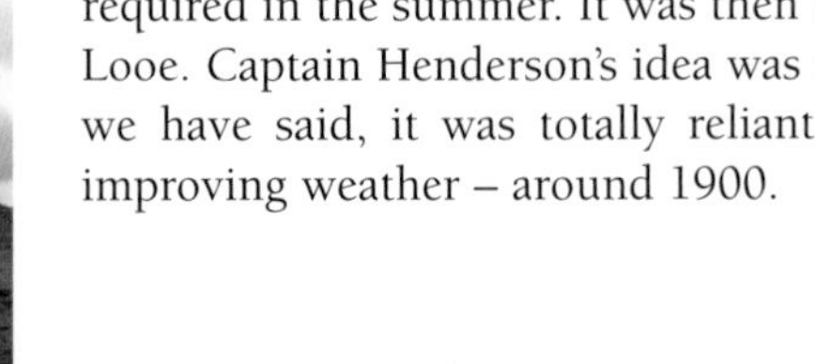

required in the summer. It was then taken down the Fowey valley to Liskeard and finally on to Looe. Captain Henderson's idea was to supply fish buyers from St Ives to Torquay. However, as we have said, it was totally reliant on severe winters. For this reason, it closed – due to improving weather – around 1900.

*****

It is Roughtor, on the other side of the moor from here, which will take centre stage in the closing section of the drama.

As I drive out towards the west coast, huge torso-less blades are turning beyond the hedgerows long before their towering slender columns come into view. A farm of wind turbines – giants that would have had Don Quixote and Sancho Panza rattling in their boots.

I cruise along Atlantic Highway, the radio blasting out Velvet Underground's *Venus in Furs*. The words seem vaguely reminiscent of Francis Davey's primeval rantings. I turn off towards the tor. Singing away, I suddenly find myself in totally unexpected surroundings. I have strayed into some sort of ghostly airfield. There's the control tower and in a few minutes I'll be clear for take-off on runway 3…

The white horse

Roughtor

At 296 metres, Davidstow used to be England's highest operational airfield. It played a vital contribution in the Allied victory in Europe though, not surprisingly, it was vulnerable to low cloud. It was mainly a post for the refuelling and loading of Flying Fortresses and Liberators attacking France. Later, when bombing switched to Germany it became the base for coastal command Wellingtons patrolling the Bay of Biscay. In February 1944, the airfield geared up for the D-Day landings. On the fateful day itself, Davidstow-based Beaufighters forced three German destroyers into Brest and away from the landing beaches, saving thousands of lives.

I make my way up to the tor. A white horse is grazing next to a stream. I decide to steer clear of the long-horns that dot the slopes. At the top, I spot a strange loculus-like formation that might be the place where Mary Yellan slept, fitfully, that night. What I really want to find, however, is the flat 'altar' stone where Joss Merlyn met his timely demise:

> *Mary saw the tall black figure of Francis Davey outlined against the sky, standing upon a wide slab like an altar, high above her head. He stood for a moment poised like a statue, his hair blowing in the wind; and then he flung out his arms as a bird throws his wings for flight, and drooped suddenly and fell; down from his granite peak to the wet dank heather and the little crumbling stones.*

Top: *Mary Yellan's bed?*

Above: *More flat 'altar' stones than you can shake a stick at!*

Longhorns on the slopes

But there is a problem – now that I am up here, I can see there are more flat 'altar' stones than you can shake a stick at…

The wind drops and there is silence except for the twittering swifts that dip and soar around me. (Brown Willy, the tor opposite, is from the Cornish, 'Bron Wennyly', for Hill of Swallows.) A white pony leisurely rubs its behind against a convenient upstanding rock. Far down in the valley a dog is barking – I think of the hounds pursuing the vicar and Mary. Brown-red butterflies alight on the remains of walls of the sixteenth century chapel that used to stand here. The view is tremendous for miles in all directions. To the north, the wind-farm I passed earlier; to the east, the tors of Dartmoor; to the west, the sea. In front of me rises the imposing mass of Brown Willy, hiding Jamaica Inn from view.

The path to Roughtor passing Brown Willy

The Inn was almost certainly a collection, storage and redistribution point for illegal merchandise. The location is perfect: not only is it incredibly remote, but it is also midway between the equally 'productive' north and south Cornish coasts.

Once seized, the merchandise needed to be 'broken down' into more practical and manageable sized quantities. Tubs of brandy would be bottled, tobacco separated into pouch-sized portions, tea transferred from chests to convenient-sized packets and cloth cut into saleable lengths. The carts arriving with new consignments and departing with the 'finished product' are what Mary hears as she lies in her bed at night.

*****

The Charlotte Dymond 'memorial' and the inscription

In the next chapter, The North Coast, I look for the location of the famous shipwreck scene and consider whether, in reality, the merchandise that passed through Jamaica Inn came from straightforward smuggling or from the much more brutal activity of wrecking.

I make my way down. The wind has risen again. A dog gallops past me with his ears blown completely inside out. On a nearby hillside, another dog guides a line of sheep along a brook. There is a curious dolmen standing alongside the bank of the stream. The inscription it bears tells the tale of a grisly murder which would have had Mr Whicher's whiskers twitching with suspicion.

Charlotte Dymond was murdered on Sunday 14 April 1844. Her body was found, a number of days later, lying in the stream just yards away from the granite obelisk. Her neck had been cut through to the bone with great force.

Charlotte was, by all accounts, a not unattractive young lady, aware of the attention that came her way and also a bit of a flirt. She had been in a relationship with another servant of the same household, Matthew Weeks. Weeks was always well turned out despite his lowly station, but physically cut rather a sorry figure. He was short, rather lame, with a pock-marked face and gapped teeth.

Accusatory fingers were immediately pointed in his direction, though there seems to have been little hard evidence to support the charges. The scapegoat was guilty long before the trial even started. On Dymond's death certificate – three and a half months before proceedings began – the cause of death was given as 'Willfully murdered by Matthew Weeks'.

The Bodmin Teetotal Festival held annually on the slopes of Roughtor, (organised by the Temperance Society and which generally ended in drunken brawls), was rechristened for that year: The Roughtor Monster Meeting. A black flag had been planted where the victim had been discovered and penny donations were received to defray the cost of erecting a monument to commemorate the heinous crime. The inscription had probably already been prepared...

Matthew Weeks was hanged, and left to hang - as was the custom - for an hour and a minute, on Monday 12 August 1844. A crowd of over 20,000 onlookers attended. Special trains had been laid on for the occasion.

The brook where Charlotte's body was found

CHAPTER 8

THE NORTH COAST

What did wrecking actually involve? If it was simply salvaging what you could from a beach after a shipwreck (which clearly was not an infrequent occurrence), then that was one thing. Wrecking as portrayed in the novel, however, using false lights to lure ships on to rocks, was a completely different matter. If it did go on, it would have often meant murder or at least omission of assistance to the victims.

The veracity of one anecdote is more or less beyond doubt – Admiral Sir Cloudesley Shovell's out-sized emerald ring almost certainly cost him his life after being shipwrecked in the Scillies in 1707. However, that is just one incident, and it was a *very big* emerald.

Breakers on the rocks

The rocky coast of Cornwall has claimed many ships

From top: *The wreck of the* Giles Lang, *1896; The wreck of the* Hansy, *1911; The* Jeune Hortense *ashore in Mount's Bay, 1888*
Right: *Shipwrecks at St Ives, 1908*

Then there are the tales of the Vicar of Morwenstow – but they are precisely that, tales. Ironically, the main source of the stories of wrecking today would seem to be a novel by the name of *Jamaica Inn*!

The lack of evidence is hardly surprising - it is highly improbable that communities living on the coast, growing up with the hardship of the sea and earning a living from it, would murder their fellow seafarers. If and when it did take place, it was going to be frowned on by society in a way that smuggling would never be and so unlikely to be bragged about or voiced around – there would be few or no records of acts such as this.

Also, this type of wrecking – by its very nature – would have to be an improvised affair, carried out by farmers or fishermen living in remote coastal areas on hand just at the right time to be able to take advantage of a ship in distress. The impossibility of advance preparation makes Joss Merlyn's Christmas Eve outing to the coast an extremely unlikely affair.

The 'business' carried out at the real-life Jamaica Inn was therefore almost certainly the result of smuggling and not wrecking.

'Business' really started to boom in the 1700s. Duties had been raised to a particularly high level on spirits, tea and tobacco in order to finance European and colonial wars. French brandy acquired at source for 5 shillings a gallon could be sold on for 5 times as much. Not surprisingly, by 1783 half of all the spirits being smuggled into England and Wales came through Devon and Cornwall. The cargo of a single trip could fetch between £2000 to £10000 on the open market at a time when a labourer might earn no more than 20 to 25 pounds a year. The North coast of Cornwall 'specialized' in rum destined for Bristol from the Caribbean, which is where perhaps the name Jamaica Inn comes from.

Tea was a prized commodity for smugglers. Many ships unloaded cargo illegally en route to their official port of destination.

Searching on eBay for images of smuggling, I come across Ogden's series of cigarette cards on the subject. They are from the Jamaica Inn period. Daphne, her husband and her father were smokers – perhaps the novel was inspired by these very cards!

These, of course, were not the only goods being contrabanded. Anything from pepper to pantaloons, chocolate to cheese, bird seed to braces was fair game. The gentler sex was also clearly a willing consumer: silks, shoes, shawls, feathers, hats, cologne and lavender were all in demand.

When it comes to the local population and moral scruples, it has to be remembered that England did not abolish the slave trade until 1806. By that time vast fortunes had been made by West Country 'merchants', from Bristol in particular. Set alongside these activities, smuggling appeared a relatively minor sin.

Having lived for a long time in Italy, I am not surprised to learn that people 'above reproach' were implicated in these criminal activities. The capital to finance 'projects' was frequently provided by prosperous and respectable members of society. The story goes, for example, that a door at the foot of the tower of Place in Fowey was permanently left ajar so that 'tributes' might be left. Or then again a rich patron might decide to throw a party for Preventive Officers at exactly the same time as a clandestine operation was taking place elsewhere.

And, as in Italy, the clergy were also often involved. Apart from vicars masterminding operations for their flock, the churches themselves provided a vast amount of storage space. At Maker, a visiting Dean was surprised to see twenty barrels of spirits lodged in the gutters of the chapel. At Duloe, the church tower actually began to sink on one side from regular overloading!

A sailing ship at Charlestown today

The authorities did eventually manage to bring the situation under control with a number of measures.

Above: *Smugglers in a cove on the Cornish Coast from a print by Thomas Rowlandson c.1810.*

Right: *Smugglers land their cargo in a hidden cove.*

Below: *Fishermen would smuggle ashore tobacco in their thigh-length boots – hence the term 'bootleg'!*

For the first of these measures, we have Adam Smith (yes, he of *The Wealth of Nations*) to thank. At the time, he was working as a customs commissioner in Scotland. Brilliant economist as he was, he saw smugglers simply as businessmen responding in the only way they could to an unfair market. (The Cornish could point out that they had called smuggling 'free trade' for years!). He was proved right – when tea duty was reduced from over 120% to just 10%, smuggling nose-dived. Reducing taxes to reasonable levels meant that the job was no longer worth the risk.

These fiscal measures were backed up, in 1809, by the establishment of the Preventive Waterguard which lead to the construction of watch houses like the one at Lansallos Bay (see chapter 10). I read somewhere that The South West Coastal Path owes a lot to the tracks beaten out by nightly patrols of coastguards. At which point it must be said that they were doing no more than following in the footsteps of the smugglers!

Things got even more problematic for the smugglers when the Coastguard Service started in 1822. Revenue cutters patrolled the sea, coastguards the shore, mounted guards inland. Francis Davey's irritated comments after his meeting on the subject in Launceston mean that we can pin down the year of the events of *Jamaica Inn* to 1821.

For those who did decide to soldier on, it meant having to resort to even greater subterfuge. Whistling a popular song, tethering animals in a prearranged fashion, a man riding a white horse or a red shirt out on the washing line – all became recognized code signs for passing on information about the authorities.

Tactics changed, too. Cargo would be stowed in false bulkheads, hollow masts and yards. Silk or lace could be hidden in children's toys or concealed in turkeys. Goods might be transported by coffin or tubs of spirits beneath skirts. Ghost stories were fabricated to keep people away from storage areas. 'Sowing the crop' (depositing barrels on the sea-bed for future collection) became a popular and safer method for getting merchandise ashore.

*****

But where exactly did *Jamaica Inn*'s wrecking scene take place? Writing this book, it has become clear that frequently du Maurier has had in mind a precise, real physical location when she tells her stories. If so, the same could hold also in this case. You will recall that Joss and his gang had travelled west to Camelford. Then, when Mary Yellan awakes we read,

> *The carriage had been abandoned in a narrow gulley-way with high banks on either side, and the horse had been taken from the traces… Her eyes strained to pierce the darkness ahead of her, down the sharp descent of the gulley-way and borne up to her on the wind came a sound at once sullen and familiar, a sound that for the first time in her life she could not welcome, but must recognize with a leap of her heart and a shiver of foreboding.*
> *It was the sound of the sea. The gully was a pathway to the shore*

Crackington Haven

There are many beaches and coves along the north coast that might match the description. Two, however, seem particularly interesting – Crackington Haven and Millook. Both were renowned for smuggling.

Surfers dwarfed by the cliffs

Crackington is a spectacular beach. Dominating the scene is the 143m high black bulk of Pencarrow point. There was once a small harbour here, importing coal and limestone from Wales and exporting slate. The Coombe Barton Inn at the head of the beach is a 300-year-old hotel originally built for the local slate quarry captain. Today it is clear that surfing has taken over from smuggling. The people walking out to the waves with their boards seem minute against the towering backdrop of the cliffs. But there is nowhere that fits the description of the gulley and so we drive north.

Millook owes its very existence to a wreck. On 7 November 1900, the *Concezione*, a 420 ton barque went aground in nearby Widemouth Bay in a north-westerly gale. It was carrying a cargo of pit props for the South Wales coal mines. The first houses here were built from the salvaged cargo.

There used to be a thriving summer holiday community here in the 1930s – the period when Daphne du Maurier might have passed through.[4] The Pellow family and their friends, apart from enjoying the swimming and the sailing, even built a tennis court on the hillside. The backend of an old Morris 10 was used as a grandstand for their annual tournament. Players would compete for the prestigious Millook Cup (in actual fact an aluminium milk saucepan).

The wooden shack on the hillock to the left as you face the sea was known as the Millook teahouse and served ice cream and refreshments. I have a brief chat with the chap who is renting it this week. It must be the most exposed, windswept holiday let in the whole of Britain!

Long before the birth of the village, however, on this beach on 11 December 1820, the famous 'Millook Incident' took place. Officers who had seized four to five hundred tubs of rum were, in their turn, attacked by smugglers who stole their boat and took back the whole of the cargo. The smuggling cutter involved had eight black gun-ports on each a side, bulwarks painted with a broad yellow stripe, a red counter with a yellow moulding, and a dark foresail with a white jib. The gangs were certainly not worried about keeping a low profile.

Looking down on Millook

Widemouth Bay

Chevron folding in the cliffs

The road out of Millook is even steeper than the one in – ancient moss-covered woods line the precipitous slope up. As we ascend, the road assumes more and more the appearance of a gulley. A descending jeep forces me to the very inside of a corner where the track seems almost vertical. The car just won't go up – it feels that any minute we might topple over backwards! I have to roll back downhill while the other car pulls into a field entrance to let me pass. And yes, the road at this point does in fact turn left, exactly as Mary Yellan describes when she clambers out of the coach.

A bit more research into the surrounding area throws up further interesting facts. In 1357, at Millook Parish Church, the then curate, Rev. William Penfound, became involved with a gang that attacked ships in the bay. After falling out with the boss, he was murdered in Poundstock church – at the altar. His restless ghost is still said to haunt the area. Did this suggest to du Maurier the fate for Francis Davey in *Jamaica Inn*?

Back towards Crackington Haven, the churchyard of St Gennys has a memorial to the shipwrecked of the Swedish brigantine *William* which in 1894, was carrying coal from Swansea to Alicante. Crackington therefore might have been the inspiration for Francis Davey's port of flight. He certainly wouldn't have chosen a big port for his getaway, he does at one point say to Mary that they are making towards 'a haven' and he even speaks of Spain as a destination.

There's more: the inhabitants of St Genny's parish used to be known by the nickname 'Wreckers and Wrestlers'. As far back as 1342, a complaint was being made to the king about their ringleader. They boarded vessels, cut cables and ropes keeping them at anchor, and let the ships wreck on the shore.

Millook could just be then the location for that famous scene, with Crackington the inspiration for Francis Davey's escape route.

Boat on the beach

Looking back on Millook

*****

We have seen that in all probability 'wrecking' as portrayed in the novel never in fact took place. Whatever the case, in addition to du Maurier's famous contribution to the corpus, there are also many other colourful stories that have grown up around the alleged activity.

By way of a postscript, here is a beauty from the *Jamaica Inn* period from the picturesque pie and pasty village of Portlemouth in South Devon.

> *One Sunday morning, the Vicar of the Parish Church was coming to the end of yet another particularly soporific sermon and the majority of the congregation had dozed off. The cold draught woke one or two – a gale was howling outside – when a man opened the church door and made his way to the pulpit and whispered in the Vicar's ear. They were all wide awake though when the Vicar started bellowing, "There's a ship on the rocks between Prawle and Pear Tree Point..." He started to tear off his encumbering vestments, surplus and robes, continuing as he did "...but let us all start fair!"*
>
> *At which point the congregation rose as one and charged headlong towards the beach... the Vicar in the lead.*

CHAPTER 9
FOWEY – READYMONEY COVE

It is still warm and sunny as we set out to walk up to Readymoney Cove. Fowey this evening has a Mediterranean feel to it. We pass the Ship Inn and turn right up the hill.

The road which leads down towards the river mouth and Readymoney is the Esplanade. It blossomed during the Victorian Period with the arrival of the railway as Fowey with its 'mild and equable climate' joined established places such as Torquay and Teignmouth as a winter watering place for those who could afford to be health-conscious. The new lodging houses and hotels not surprisingly chose to distance themselves from the more insalubrious and dilapidated cottages along North Street at the other end of the town.

The Haven

On the left, you can peek into dining rooms of houses with the most fabulous views over the river. Fabulous prices too, most probably. Soon we come to a house which stands out from all the rest. The verandah has something vaguely Indian about it.

This is The Haven. A plaque on the wall tells us that Sir Arthur Quiller-Couch lived here from 1892 to 1944. Du Maurier had been introduced to Q, an eminent literary professor and author of the *Troy Town* stories, over tea at Jesus College, Cambridge soon after the acquisition of Ferryside. She would become a regular guest for Sunday dinner and it was one of the few times she would change out of trousers: she says she felt she almost needed to curtsey in his presence. She became firm friends with his daughter, Foy, and it was with her that she first explored Bodmin Moor and Jamaica Inn. As we shall see in a later chapter it was Foy who asked Daphne du Maurier, shortly after her father's death, to finish his work, *Castle Dor,* just as Q had finished R.L. Stevenson's *St Ives.*

Memorial plaque

Next, on the right, is the impressive pile of the Fowey Hotel, built in 1882, where according to Angela du Maurier, the family lunched on their very first day in the town.

The Fowey Hotel

The wall on the left is now running along precipitous cliffs. Growing out of chinks in the bare rock are deep pink tufts of Q's favourite valerian (the Pride of Fowey, as he called it). These cliffs would have made great defences for the medieval town but must cause a few worries to the houses now perched on the edge of the chasm as the frequent evidence of bolstering up of the cliff faces testifies.

On the corner where the road curves to descend to Readymoney Cove stands Point Neptune.

It was William Rashleigh who, realising the resort potential of this part of Fowey, gave Readymoney the residential feel it has today. On the site of an eighteenth century gun emplacement, he built Point Neptune in the Italianate marine villa style. The stables and coach house were situated down at the head of the Cove. He chose in fact to live here in preference to Menabilly, his country estate. He is buried a stone's throw away on the other side of the cove in the rather bizarre mausoleum that he erected as a final resting place for himself and his wife.

The property was purchased by Dawn French and Lenny Henry a few years back. For the du Maurier fan, however, the real attraction of the place lies not inside but at the very entrance.

Readymoney, a postcard dated July 1913

Theses gates are the originals that stood at the beginning of the carriage drive to Menabilly – you can clearly see their swirling centre pattern in the sepia photo on page 130 of du Maurier's *Enchanted Cornwall*.

These are the same rusted spokes through which the dreaming Mrs de Winter peers at the abandoned lodge and the twisting, strangely overgrown drive at the opening of *Rebecca*. These are the spokes that Daphne du Maurier also peered through, nervously expectant, that very first time she ventured up to Menabilly. These are the spokes that present-day fans of famous television personalities can't peer through as they have backed the gates with black material.

Just a little further on down the slope you come to Fowey's only real beach – Readymoney. The origin of the name comes from 'Redeman', that is, a ford of stepping stones. This was obviously a well known crossing point in antiquity.

Daphne du Maurier came to live in the bungalow at the head of the beach – 8 Readymoney Cove – in April 1942. (She could not move back into Ferryside as it had been requisitioned by the US navy).

Point Neptune gates

Readymoney Cove

Above: *The raft, Readymoney Cove*

Above right: *Du Maurier House, Readymoney*

At the outset of the war she had moved her family to Hertfordshire, to a Lutyens house owned by a couple called Puxley, ironically as it turned out, so that she could be closer to her husband, Tommy, who was stationed in the area. He had been given command of a new division of glider-borne paratroopers. This was in preparation for what would come to be called Operation Market Garden – and its famous 'Bridge Too Far'.

Almost as soon as she arrives, she is ominously writing in a letter that whereas the wife is rushed off her feet with her work for the WVS and the Red Cross, the husband Henry Puxley, is a wistfully wandering sensitive type who plays the piano divinely and looks like the young Compton Mackenzie.

She absents herself briefly when her son Kits is born and then moves back again. Interestingly, and yet typically, she can become quite jealous of the attention her husband receives playing tennis from a family of young girls during a brief spell of leave at the house, whilst, at the same time, falling head over heels for Christopher Puxley (she has now renamed him as Christopher and herself as Jane(t) after the characters in *The Loving Spirit*). She is wooed by his savoir faire and his exquisite playing of Chopin. Her favourite is the 24th Prelude – a highly difficult piece which bears witness to his pianistic talent. The work is known as 'The Storm' due to its tempestuous quality.

And a storm certainly was brewing. Du Maurier's way of coping with the new emotions she was experiencing (rather shamefully as she admitted) was to write. Christopher would be the peg on which she could hang her new swashbuckling, ultra-romantic novel, *Frenchman's Creek*. Puxley would be the model for the daring yet sensitive French pirate who would whisk the heroine off her feet.

In the novel she perversely mixes the memories of her honeymoon spent at the creek with her new-found feelings for Puxley. Then, behaving, by all accounts, quite recklessly and with an almost blatant insouciance, she is discovered 'in flagrante' in Christopher's arms by his wife, Paddy. And so she moves into Readymoney.

Frenchman's Creek ends with Dona Colomb bidding goodbye to the Frenchman on the shores of Looe Pool and returning to her husband. The reality was slightly messier. Christopher Puxley would travel down to see her, staying at the Fowey Hotel, and they would meet secretly at an old coastguard's hut along the coast (see chapter 10). It is presumably these occasions that her daughter Flavia refers to in her biography, 'There were days when Bing had to be free of us'.

Finally, one is tempted to say, when Christopher Puxley no longer served any purpose, he is discarded. Daphne writes in 1962 to Oriel Malet

Readymoney, postcard dated August 13th 1947

Frenchman's Creek, *2nd impression October 1941*

Below: *Lilies in front of the house*

Below right: *Daphne du Maurier lived here*

> *So great was my Gondal-peg urge towards the man in whose house we were staying that Frenchman's Creek absolutely tore along! (Anything less like the Frenchman, really, than the poor man, there couldn't be, but I gondalled him into it and saw him that way!).*

It is as if, either consciously or unconsciously, she saw herself as standing outside the canons of conventional morality.

There is more. I am holding now my 1941 copy of *Frenchman's Creek* in its original distinctive Gollancz bright yellow dust cover. Because of paper rationing for the war effort, it is gossamer light and proudly boasts on its spine that, notwithstanding this, it still contains 80,000 words. Her soldier-husband was working all the hours that God sent to protect his country. She was having an affair, which inspired her to write a book. She is found out by his partner but still goes ahead and publishes. She dedicates the book to Paddy (the cuckolded wife) and Christopher. She told her daughter that the Frenchman was a mixture of her father and Christopher.

*****

The house is almost as close to the beach as you could get. You get the impression that at high tide you could pull your boat up right into the front garden. Flavia Leng's biography tells us that, back then, Readymoney was painted white with black window-sills, with a mass of pretty yellow roses climbing across the front. At the back of the house was a large garden with wide lawns and a shrubbery with a little stream running through part of it. A tennis court was tucked behind a beech hedge at the far end.

The back garden

At that time, with the fear of imminent German invasion, huge iron bars some six metres high had been built in the water of the cove to ward off enemy landing craft, becoming partly submerged when the tide was in.

Inside the house was rather dark, except for the upstairs bedroom which her mother had. This is presumably the window directly above the commemorative plaque.

Coincidentally, a couple of weeks later, I am thumbing through the *Western Morning News* when I see the house in the Property section. 'Now available on the open market for the first time in over 50 years having been a long-cherished family home'. The 1.25 acre garden still looks wonderful, but they have sadly done away with the tennis court. The asking price is a snip at just £1,650,000. If, that is, you are one of those who has to hand that sort of ready money.

Out for an evening cruise

The cove appears twice in the novels. In *The Loving Spirit,* Christopher joyously returns to Plyn after many years in exile in London only to be greeted at the station by the tragic news that his father, Joseph, is dead. His cap and coat have been found washed up on 'Pennytinny' sands, his boat cast adrift with her boards broken.

On a lighter, more melodramatic note, the beach here is where, in *Frenchman's Creek*, after the daring raid on Fowey, Dona scrambles out onto the rocks jutting out from the cove to warn the *Merry Fortune* of the impending danger from St Catherine's fort. After what seems like an age, she eventually recognises Pierre Blanc's insistent gull-cry and spots his small boat.

She is promptly rescued amid the roar, crashes, flashes, splashes, deafening reports and splintering wood of cannon fire, to be delivered, literally in the nick of time, safe and sound - albeit slightly scratched, to her beloved Frenchman.

As we walk back, the electric gates of Point Neptune swing open. Moments later, Dawn French, wearing a head scarf, passes us in her Range Rover. I am reminded of a story one of the shopkeepers told me about how Daphne du Maurier used to come into town and go to the bank and nobody took any notice. Probably no one from outside the town would have even recognised her. How different in this *Hello* magazine era for the Dawn Frenches of this world!

We make our way back to Fowey as the sun is going down. The setting rays are illuminating the slates of the roofs of Polruan. A passage from *The Cornish Coast and Moor* written back in 1912 by A.G. Folliott-Stokes comes to mind. Admittedly, the prose is of a shade perilously close to his 'plum-coloured' woods but I still think it renders the idea:

> *The sun had set an hour ago, and the long June day was coming to a close. A green Italian brigantine was lying under the opposite wooded hill, now a rich plum colour in the gathering gloom. Polruan rose tier on tier of old-world houses framed by the elms. Overhead was a sky of violet shot with gold. It was a wonderful twilight and a most wonderful picture. But there was another glory yet to come. As we gazed, the moon, first like a golden bow and then in full-orbed splendour, rose slowly over the roofs of Polruan and completed the witchery of the coming night.*

Looking out to Punches Cross

CHAPTER 10

LANTEGLOS CHURCH, LANTIC & LANTIVET BAY

Today I drive to see the church at Lanteglos. We turn down the road to Pont with the sunlight streaming through the trees. Clouds of golden midges hang in the still air. At the bottom of the valley, there is a brook. Tree ferns and enormous clumps of gunnera are backlit by the morning sun.

To the right there is a mill pond and, across the water, the bridge we stopped at the other day at the head of Pont Pill. And, as the road turns to mount the hill, a path leads up through the trees to the church – the one Daphne du Maurier would have taken on the morning of her wedding.

Top: *Tree ferns at Pont*

Above: *The path up to the church*

Left: *Looking across the mill pond at low tide*

The tower in the sunlight

Her mother had pressed her light blue serge suit the night before and they had risen early to catch the tide. They were greeted by bunting hung out by the villagers on the cottages opposite Ferryside.

There weren't many guests present. Daphne, for her part, had engineered it so that her sisters would be away travelling in Italy when they heard the news of the imminent wedding. Tommy, strangely, on his side had nobody.

They left in two boats. The groom and the Hunkins followed behind in *Ygdrasil*. The *Cora Ann* led the way with Daphne, her mother, father and Geoffrey, her father's brother.

And an odd little wedding party it must have been. One can only imagine the atmosphere. Relations had been strained with her mother for years, maybe because of the almost morbid attention the daughter received from the father. As for Gerald, he had most theatrically burst into tears when he read the engagement letter, declaiming that it wasn't fair.

And Geoffrey – who had been more or less besotted with Daphne since they had held hands under the cover on Thurlestone beach – why on earth, was Geoffrey invited? Was it some sort

Lanteglos church

of perverse prank on Daphne's part? Or did he just turn up unawares on another of his 'brotherly' visits? Du Maurier comments that he made the usual best man jokes, which fell rather flat. One dreads to think what they were.

But you get the feeling that one person – Daphne – would not have been overly worried by all the underlying history, in fact, would have seen it as all quite amusing. In any case, she was already confusing fact and fiction in her life. As she wrote in *Growing Pains* "by boat it must be, like the young couple in *The Loving Spirit*".

The wedding breakfast that day would literally be sausages and bacon cooked on board *Ygdrasil*. Then it was off down the coast to the Helford River and Frenchman's Creek, pausing only mid-estuary as they left Fowey to pick up the bottle of home-made sloe gin that the Quiller-Couches rowed out to hand to them.

She was embarking on a voyage which at times would get stormy but she would prove that she wasn't the type to jump ship. She would demonstrate that she had a strong sense of duty, if not to her husband, then to her children. A sense of duty which she would also transfer to her heroine Dona Columb in *Frenchman's Creek*. A quality which would steer her and Tommy, eventually, into the calmer waters of old age.

The entrance to the church

*****

We walk through the open gate into the churchyard. The path to the south door is lined with tombstones. The first two or three bear familiar names. They give an instant snapshot of what life must have been like in Polruan in the nineteenth century.

The Salts were an important family in the town. The men were the Trinity Pilots for the port. Christopher Slade had married Jane Salt whose father also owned the Russell Inn.

John and Hannah Salt lived to the ripe old age of 70 and 76 years old. Then next to them comes the shock – a headstone for their children: Mary who died at 5 months, Joseph at 15 years, Bernice and James at just 11 months (Christopher and Jane Slade would also lose their first son in the month he was born). Infant mortality rates were terrifyingly high. It's difficult to even start to imagine the dramas these few lines contain. The first child buried here was born, and died, when Hannah was only 15 and John was 26.

Others reveal that so many of the men were killed at sea, Master Mariners among them, at very young ages, leaving their wives to mourn the rest of their lives alone. One stone contains two such tragedies: the husbands dying at sea at the ages of 40 and 32, the wives outliving them to 66 and 86 years respectively.

Opposite - left to right: *John and Hannah Salt's gravestone. The headstone of their children. The tomb of Master Mariners, William Allen.*

Jane and Christopher Slade's headstone and the headstone amongst the ivy

At the foot of the stone, a poignant comment;

Brief life is here our portion
Brief sorrow, short lived care
The life that knows no ending
The tearless life – is there.

But where is Jane's headstone, the one that du Maurier had come up here to visit when researching the book and again on the day she finished the manuscript to "make some sort of thanksgiving"? I have to go back to the car to find the photo in Jane Doe's book. It is from the round-topped shape and the engraved disc that I eventually manage to identify it. The inscription is almost totally obscured by yellowish-orange lichen. But there it is – to the left and back near the wall as you go in. Jane and Christopher Slade.

The heavy oak door of the church creaks open. The interior of cream stone is beautifully understated and suffused with a soft yellow light. There is a wonderful description of the effect in *The Loving Spirit* as Janet sits in the church the day that Joseph, master of his first ship, sails out of Plyn.

> *The setting sun caught the western windows in a beam of light. She knew this same beam would cross the path of the ship that sailed away. The little church was hushed and peaceful. Centuries old, it still held the presence of those folk who had knelt there in years gone by. The stones were worn with the knees of humble people, now in their graves, their names long buried and forgotten. Those who worshipped there beside Janet would one day in their turn come to the same unbroken silence and rest.*

The altar, Lanteglos Church

There *is* a marvellous silence, with just one sound – but from outside – the gentle lowing of the cows up on the hill.

Later that evening I phone the vicar, Louise, to ask her if the wedding certificate of du Maurier is kept in the church. She says she will get her expert on historical records to call me back. She has such an infectious personality that I ask if she isn't perhaps the female vicar in the BBC series *Island Parish*. No, that's not me, she replies – I would have put my foot in it in every episode! Delightful – her parishioners are lucky.

The certificate is in the Cornwall Record Office in Truro, but no matter. I have seen the place and that is enough.

Cows on the hillside outside the church

*****

We are close to the coast, near the beaches of Lantic and Lantivet Bay. I want to find the watchman's house, the lonely hut perched on the edge of the cliff looking out to sea, which was rented by du Maurier at one point.

My National Trust leaflet suggests that she used the hut for writing. The present owner disagrees. It does seem a long way to come just to put pen to paper…

I take the wrong route through a tree-covered tunnel, deep in mud. A couple are walking in the same direction parallel to me in the adjacent field. They are arguing violently in some Eastern European language, maybe Czech. I feel I need to cough just to indicate my presence. As I have just finished my book on Agatha Christie, the infinite plot variations of the situation start immediately coursing through my brain.

Emerging out on to the headland the sky is a leaden grey. I decide that the hut must be to the left and I strike out. After 15 minutes of quite strenuous hills and valleys, walls and stiles, I am becoming more and more perplexed by the presence of a church steeple on the skyline ahead of me which the Ordnance men have carelessly omitted from their maps.

All of a sudden, the sun breaks through the clouds. Although I am completely alone on the cliff-top, I do actually

Lantivet Bay

whisper, "Wow!" The illuminated headlands have become a deep saturated emerald green, the sea a rich sapphire, the border between the two edged by a brilliant white line of surf. The mica or schist in the rocks of the cove below me is making them sparkle in the sunlight. Right off into the distance is cove after headland after cove after headland. At that moment it is possibly the most beautiful stretch of coast I have ever seen.

I turn round to take in the full panorama. I look back along the way I have come. There on the distant cliffs, nestling in the bracken, is a little whitewashed hut...

So I am now standing above Lantivet Bay not Lantic Bay (yes, there were signs but these Cornish names are all so confusing). The steeple is then in fact on the map, it's Lansallos church.

A sparkling cove

I start to retrace my steps. The couple are still there on a bench but have opened a bottle of beer and seemed to have patched things up. I bet they are annoyed to find anyone around here on a weekday out of season. It's the sort of place you would come to be alone for a good talk or, well, just to be alone.

As I approach, the hut has disappeared again. Then I come to a steep, almost hidden, path leading down through the gorse and ferns. 50 metres or so further down on the right is a gate secured by a piece of blue rope. The hut is set back against the cliff, with a scrubby piece of grass in front. A blue director's chair is sitting in the middle of it.

The watchman's hut - back along the cliffs

The path to the hut

It would seem that the present occupant is in residence. I have read a lot in my Daphne research about trespassing over the last few weeks and I would dearly like to get a shot of the inside the house, through a window. But the front is obscured by bushes and I would be standing in front of the building before I realised there was someone at home. Best not. I carry on down to where an impossibly steep flight of steps leads down to a small cove. Now that is a definite 'No'.

The Watchman's hut had been built as a coastguard lookout in 1835, following the so-called Lantic Hill Affair. The *Daniel and William*, a passenger boat also involved in the 'free trade' movement, landed a cargo of brandy which was then hidden to wait for collection. The following day 100 or so men took part in the back-breaking process of carrying the tubs up the 300 foot cliff.

As it happened, two coastguards were having a smoke behind a hedge at the top and heard what was going on. Coastguard Stevens remained to keep an eye on things while Coastguard Harper went back to Polruan for reinforcements. It says a lot about the type of volunteers coerced into this type of activity when you think that, skirmish over, the six coastguards faced with over a hundred smugglers had managed nevertheless to apprehend five!

The hut nestles in the bracken

Pencarrow Head

In all, 484 gallons of brandy were recovered. However, the preventive men hadn't reckoned on the closeness of the communities at the time. Despite being caught red-handed and having knocked unconscious one of the officers, a jury of twelve found them not guilty. This was perhaps the origin of the saying that a Cornish jury will never convict a Cornishman.

During the Second World War this area was off-limits to civilians. Du Maurier, however, was willing to run the risk to spend time with her friend 'Christopher' Puxley. Farther away from prying eyes you could not wish to get. If she didn't wax lyrical here while writing her manuscripts, then she certainly waxed passionate over Christopher.

I climb up on to Pencarrow head, an outcrop of rock where the Grenvilles had a summer house. As I walk along the ridge over Lantic Bay a kestrel is keeping one step ahead of me flying in a looping blanket-stitch motion along the top of the cliff. On the steep slopes ponies are grazing and a family has scrambled down to the beach and are walking along the water's edge.

Lantic Bay

Du Maurier mentions the spot in *Vanishing Cornwall*. She was 21 at the time. It was a dull day and she was fishing for pollack with a Cornish boatman, presumably Harry Adams. The fish aren't biting and she happens to mention that they would have done better to stay ashore and go rabbiting instead. At which point he shakes his head, pulls in the lines sighing "We'll catch no fish today". Mentioning a hare or rabbit while at sea is apparently, in Cornwall, one of the unluckiest things you can do.

The bays are clearly signposted!

Years later she would remember the bay in *Frenchman's Creek*. This is the place where the Frenchman, Dona and the crew land when they make their incursion into Fowey to capture, amongst other things, Godolphin's wig.

Just the one field of cows to negotiate and I am back on the road. Then it's a ten-minute walk back to the car.

A couple stop and wind down the window. They are completely lost and have been looking for Lantivet Bay for more than 20 minutes.

"Lantivet Bay?" I reply, knowledgeably moving the stress to the second syllable.

"Carry straight on for half a mile and there's a car-park on the left. The path to the beach is just across the road. You can't miss it – it's clearly signposted."

It is said with the assurance of one who has been walking these lanes for years.

A.L. Rowse would have been proud of me.

CHAPTER 11
THE HELFORD RIVER & FRENCHMAN'S CREEK

Du Maurier said so herself – *Frenchman's Creek* was her one and only out-and-out 'romantic' novel. "A romance with a capital R", she wrote to Victor Gollancz.

There were also hints that she had reservations. In one letter she describes it as "more or less pure Jeffery Farnol". Farnol was a prolific author of Mills & Boon-type novels with swashbuckling heroes and swooning heroines who had already slipped out of vogue at the time she was writing.

Yet taken for what it is – a lighthearted pirate adventure – the pages flick by with the usual ease. I remember reading it 'tout d'un trait' one afternoon on a sun-lounger in the garden. It has certainly proved popular over the years, and is still regularly up there in the top three with *Rebecca* and *Jamaica Inn*.

This is one of the locations I've been really looking forward to. Perhaps it's because it's so much more off the beaten track than the others, perhaps it's because of those famous descriptions that open the novel.

Boat moored in Frenchman's Creek

Opposite: *The creek at Helford*

> *The solitary yachtsman who leaves his yacht in the open roadstead of Helford, and goes exploring up river in his dinghy on a night in midsummer, when the night-jars call, hesitates when he comes upon the mouth of the creek, for there is something of mystery about it even now, something of enchantment. Being a stranger, the yachtsman looks back over his shoulder to the safe yacht in the roadstead, and to the broad waters of the river, and he pauses, resting on his paddles, aware suddenly of the deep silence of the creek, of its narrow twisting channel, and he feels – for no reason known to him – that he is an interloper, a trespasser in time. He ventures a little way along the left bank of the creek, the sound of the blades upon the water seeming over-loud and echoing oddly amongst the trees on the farther bank, and as he creeps forward the creek narrows, the trees crowd yet more thickly to the water's edge, and he feels a spell upon him, fascinating, strange, a thing of queer excitement not fully understood.*

The nightjar and its call really fascinated du Maurier. Will I get to see or hear one? Probably not – as the name implies this elusive bird is a creature of the night, or at best the dusk. Also my recently acquired *Birds of Cornwall and the Isles of Scilly* contains a photo of every single bird to be seen in the county, with one notable exception. I am not holding out much hope.

We leave Helston and start to skirt the perimeter fence of RNAS Culdrose. Twenty minutes later we are still skirting the perimeter fence of RNAS Culdrose. It is difficult to believe as we drive past the interminable air-base that at this point we are only minutes away from one of the most unspoilt, uncontaminated stretches of countryside in Cornwall.

Below: *House at Helford*

Below right: *Garage at Helford*

But the road does turn off eventually towards Gweek. Gweek was, at the beginning of the fourteenth century, the main port for Helston. The quay in the centre of the village is clearly still a thriving boatyard and the signs tell me that the village is also home to a seal sanctuary.

A Lutyenesque house

Once out of the village, we are soon driving through secluded woods. We follow the banks of small streams, cross bridges at the heads of creeks and pass signs to Trelowarren where du Maurier's friend, Clara Vyvyan lived. Within ten minutes, we are descending the steep road into Helford.

There has been a village here since 1230. The name is probably a combination of the Cornish 'heyl' meaning estuary and the English 'ford'. In the nineteenth century, it was a thriving fishing community, but most of the fish cellars have now been incorporated into private houses.

The village is idyllic. This is the peaceful, bucolic backwater that Mary Yellan, after the death of her mother, was forced to give up for the 'hospitality' of Jamaica Inn. This is the maternal, womb-like world that she has to exchange for the violent, masculine territory of Bodmin Moor.

We pass the inn. The Shipwright's Arms dates back to the eighteenth century and would have made the most of trade from passengers waiting for the ferry. Up above the track, across the field to the left, is an interesting, white Lutyenesque house built by the architect J.A. Campbell.

As we come to Helford Point, the vista opens up down towards the sea. It is a magnificently broad expanse of shimmering, deep blue water. At the mouth of the estuary large ships are sheltering or waiting for orders to continue up the channel.

For the moment there seems to be no sign of the ferry. The ferry boat company, I read, is based across the river in Helford Passage so that will be our next port of call.

Large ship at the mouth of the river

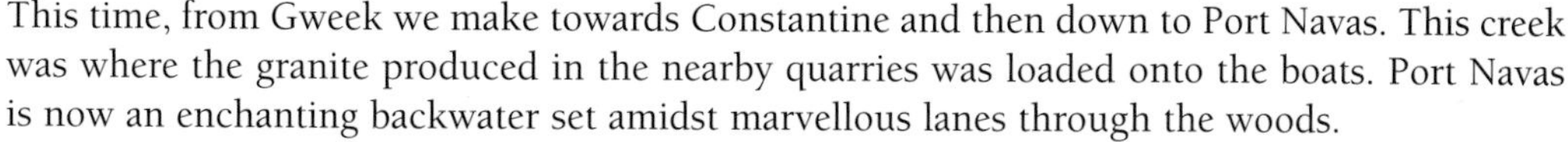

This time, from Gweek we make towards Constantine and then down to Port Navas. This creek was where the granite produced in the nearby quarries was loaded onto the boats. Port Navas is now an enchanting backwater set amidst marvellous lanes through the woods.

There has been a ferry linking Helford passage to Helford since medieval times, if not earlier. Records show that it was owned by the (ubiquitous) Bishops of Exeter. The ferry consisted of a rowing boat up until 1929 when a motor was added. There was also a horse boat which ran from nearby Bar Beach. Wagons and carts were loaded on the boat while the intrepid animals had to swim behind on a long rope.

The Ferryboat Inn and surrounding cottages all still belonged to the coastguard until around 1890. The original hotel building was, however, knocked down in the mid 1930s.

I want to see if I can charter a boat from the Helford River boat company for half an hour to take me up to Frenchman's Creek. The kiosk is unmanned so I walk up through the gallery to Sarah's craft shop. She radios her husband and my trip is sorted. As it is not too busy, we will be able to take the ferry itself upriver for a quick trip.

As we motor upstream, my captain, Nick, explains to me that apart from tourism, the main industry on the river at present is the oyster beds.

The beds are leased from the Duchy of Cornwall. Native oyster brood is brought in from the Fal and Solent. It is then left to mature on the beds in the river. Harvesting starts in August ready for the start of the season which runs from 1st September to mid-May. The oysters are sorted, graded and rested on the foreshore at Port Navas. Next they are cleansed in tanks of cool water

Above: *Port Navas creek*

Left: *Helford River above Port Navas*

Helford Passage, 1907

Helford River boat hire kiosk

Oyster beds

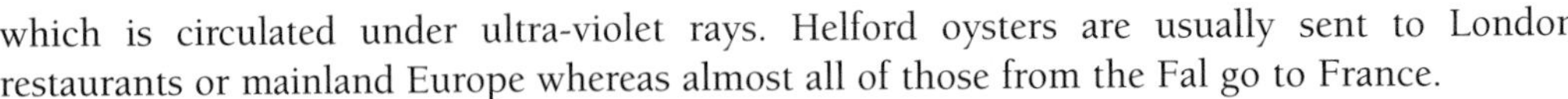
which is circulated under ultra-violet rays. Helford oysters are usually sent to London restaurants or mainland Europe whereas almost all of those from the Fal go to France.

It's good to see such a traditional activity prospering more than ever. The history goes way back. Coastal Celtic settlements of the third century BC show the collection of oysters for food. For Phoenician traders and Roman settlers they were a familiar and welcome addition to the menu. Turkish pirates were even reputed to have targeted Cornish oysters!

In less than ten minutes Nick tells me that we are about to turn into Frenchman's Creek. I have a real feeling of anticipation.

Perhaps it's the effect of the trees growing right down to and over the water's edge, but it feels as if the banks are closing in almost as soon as we enter. On the left is a cottage which can be rented from the National Trust and on the opposite side a little quay which is still used by oyster fishermen. This must be the quay where Jean-Benoit Aubery cooked the fish they had caught on an open fire for Dona.

Entering Frenchman's Creek

House on the left bank

The banks are a graveyard of abandoned vessels in various stages of decay. Dead trees also lie drowned at the water's edge. Their bare, twisted and contorted branches lie half-submerged in the water like the tentacles of mythical sea creatures. It is clear that a trip up here, alone in a rowing boat, on a moonlit night, would be eerie to say the least!

Old fishing quay

Of course, this was not only the setting for *Frenchman's Creek* but also for Daphne and Tommy's honeymoon in *Ygdrasil*. It was said to be one of his favourite books, reminding him, as it did, of his first days of married life. And I suppose, to a certain extent, she used those memories as inspiration for the book.

Du Maurier was, in fact, when she wrote *Frenchman's Creek* using, with Q's permission, the title of one of his short stories, published in 1905. The story purports to explain how the creek came to get its name. It's a comical tale with more than a hint of farce. Apparently, Captain Bligh (of Mutiny on the Bounty fame) is sent by the Admirality to chart the river. On his way to his assignment he shares a stage coach with the local vicar's wife, and as she is annoying him he decides to carry on his conversation with his friend in French. The story is taking place at a time when there was heightened fear of a French invasion and the woman is terrified. One thing

Wreck

The banks close in

leads to another and Bligh is 'captured' by the villagers as he swims naked at the top of the creek. Hence the name.

We come up to a pontoon in the middle of the river. Here my skipper tells me that, as there is a submerged fallen tree just up from here which is not visible from the boat, it would be dangerous to proceed any further. Understandable. But why does he then have to add, cruelly, that just round the next bend the creek opens out into a most spectacular pool that is really worth seeing?

What is even more frustrating is that this must be the 'secret anchorage' for *La Mouette* in the creek just below Navron House.

> *The cable rattled with a hollow sound in the deep pool beneath the trees, and the ship swung round to meet the last of the flood tide, and suddenly from nowhere came a swan and his mate, like two white barges sailing in company, and following them three cygnets, soft and brown. They went away down the creek, leaving a wake behind them as a vessel would, and presently all was snugged down for the night and the decks deserted, the smell of cooking came from the galley forward, and the low murmur of voices as the men talked in the fo'c'sle.*

The end of the journey

We turn round and make our way back.

Looking at the maps of the creek, the location of Navron House would be at Kestle, where there has been a settlement since the fourteenth century. Kestle Barton looks like the most likely candidate for the house itself. Du Maurier goes into considerable detail about the layout of Navron. Two pillars that formed the entrance to the house have now been incorporated into the modern barn. The E-shaped plan of the demolished house bears little likeness to the present day farmhouse. Of the formal garden and the park there is no trace.

Leaving Frenchman's Creek

There is also a steep track from Kestle down to the creek where there is another enchanting property that can be rented from the Landmark Trust. This is the Cuckoo Cottage that Clara Vyvyan writes of in her book *The Helford River*. From here it is possible to walk the entire length of the east bank of Frenchman's Creek.

Unfortunately, Kestle and the cottage, too, will have to be for another visit. Living in Devon, Helford is frustratingly at the extreme limit of our daily incursions into Cornwall and we need to be getting back.

Back to Helford Passage

The ferry stage at Helford

The Lady Hamilton

Stars on the water

As a honeymoon destination, Frenchman's Creek was certainly a most romantic setting, especially with an arrival by boat, and what with the pub down at Helford and the Ferryboat Hotel at Helford Passage, they were not that far away from civilisation.

As the historians point out, too, despite its reputation as the perfect hideaway for French pirate ships, with its four fish and oyster quays it was, in centuries gone by, possibly one of the busier creeks on the river!

Nick is concerned that there may well be people waiting by now at Helford for the ferry. High up on the fields on the opposite bank an enormous line of seagulls and crows follow the furrow of a ploughing tractor. In mid-stream another scene from *The Birds* is played out as the *Lady Hamilton* – an oyster fishing boat – sorts through its catch to the intense interest of the assembled flock.

We pick up a group of charming ladies at the ferry-stop and then it is back across to the Ferryboat Hotel to mull over the day's proceedings with a glass of chilled wine.

The terrace is still basking in the warm October sun. The boats moored in the roadstead doze as thousands of glinting stars dance on the surface of the water. The Helford River and Frenchman's Creek have lived up to expectations.

CHAPTER 12
POLRIDMOUTH

At about 2.30 pm on Thursday afternoon, 16th January, the "Romanie" left Fowey for Par when a very heavy sea was running and a strong wind blowing from the south-east. As soon as she got out of Fowey harbour mouth, she encountered difficulties. She lost steerage way owing to the choppiness of the sea and the fact that her propeller was frequently out of water, rendering the steering ineffective. Realising that he could not make Par, the Captain decided to return to Fowey and was in the act of doing so when he ran into Pridmouth Bay. Here both anchors were dropped but the vessel swung round head to wind, dragging her anchors, and ran onto the rocks in the Bay. Her engines were kept running and the captain succeeded in getting her off the rocks, but she was driven back again.

As soon as the rockets of distress were sent up the Fowey lifeboat lost no time in leaving the harbour for the vessel, under J. Grose, the coxswain.

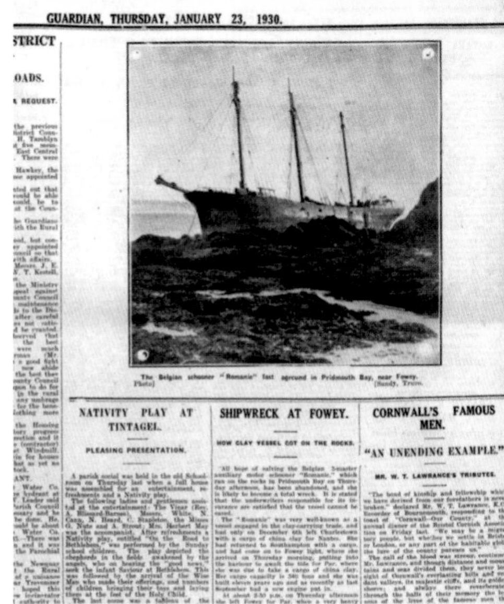

GUARDIAN, THURSDAY, JANUARY 23, 1930.

The Belgian schooner "Romanie" fast aground in Pridmouth Bay, near Fowey.
Photo] [Sandy, Truro.

NATIVITY PLAY AT TINTAGEL.

PLEASING PRESENTATION.

SHIPWRECK AT FOWEY.

HOW CLAY VESSEL GOT ON THE ROCKS.

CORNWALL'S FAMOUS MEN.

"AN UNENDING EXAMPLE."

MR. W. T. LAWRANCE'S TRIBUTES.

So the *Cornish Guardian* of 23 January 1930 reported the shipwreck of the 34 metre, 248 ton china-clay vessel, *Romanie*.

The maroons were heard back in Fowey by the young Daphne du Maurier as she worked on the fourth part of *The Living Spirit*. The sound and commotion made a deep impression on her. Although *Growing Pains* makes it clear that Part Three had been finished in the previous November, it is tempting to think that, after this incident, she went back and rewrote the last pages, perhaps the most dramatic moment of the book, which takes Christopher, bent on the destruction of evil Uncle Phillip via the three crashing reports of the lifeboat call, to his own tragic death in a matter of minutes.

She walked up to the cove the following day to scenes of people scavenging amongst the flotsam. Although she does not mention it directly in *Growing Pains*, she took the whole wrecking sequence, not even changing the name of the ship, and transferred it to the Baie des Trespasses on the French coast for the pivotal scene at the heart of *I'll Never Be Young Again*

Polridmouth, old postcards

when Jake is drowned. The sight of the debris on the beach and a brightly coloured magazine lying in a pool, would serve to open Part Two of the same novel.

She let the incident of the wreck of the *Romanie* 'brew' in her head for some 6 or 7 years before realizing it could be the key scene of her most famous work: the beginning of the unravelling of Maxim's dark secret. Once again it is the distress rockets exploding in the night sky which will divert the action away from what might have been a very different outcome. Mrs Danvers had been on the point of edging Mrs de Winter to her death from Rebecca's bedroom window. And thus it was that the diver on inspecting the wreck, would make the chilling discovery of the other small boat, with occupant, lying on the sandy bed of the shallow bay.[5]

Paying for the car park

We park the car in the field for Polridmouth beach. I hadn't really looked at the topography of the headland at this point. I, of course, remembered du Maurier's famous account of her attempts to reach Menabilly, walking for what seemed miles down the overgrown drive without ever even reaching the house. Later I look out my Ordnance Survey map and see how close we had been to Menabilly – we had walked within a couple of hundred metres of the house, it was just over there behind the trees. It is only if you approach the house from Four Turnings that you encounter the long funnel of woods and the winding carriage drive which have become so famous. Approached from other directions, the house is not far from the public highway,

We come to Menabilly Barton, visited together with the 'Barton Acres' (the farmland of the headland) by Rachel and Phillip soon after she arrives in his life in *My Cousin Rachel*. A milk churn is placed at the entrance asking for contributions from those who have used the car-park. The farm is starkly lit – half in bright sunlight, half in dark shadows. Coming towards us up the lane is a farmer with bare torso, dropped muscular shoulders and the leathery, tanned skin of

Menabilly Barton

The path down to Polridmouth

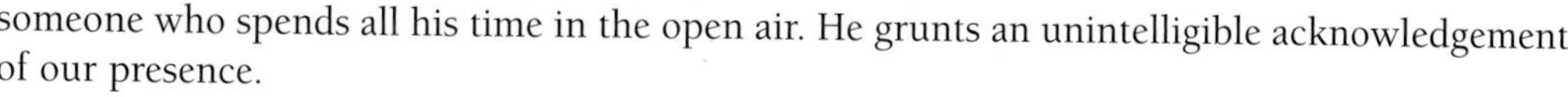

someone who spends all his time in the open air. He grunts an unintelligible acknowledgement of our presence.

The air is hot and thick with the buzzing of insects. Cows peer through gaps in the hedge and scrutinise our passage. There have been cows everywhere we have been. Driving down to Cornwall there had even been special 'bovine' traffic lights to let herds cross the main roads. Across the ploughed fields stands the Gribbin.

Du Maurier tells that this is where, seeing a cloud of screaming seagulls circling above a tractor, the short story *The Birds* was first hatched. (Today, the Hitchcock extras are still alive and pecking. My late aunt Stephanie was attacked on St Ives harbourside while eating her fish and chips and spent most of her day trip in A & E with tetanus jabs and stitches to boot.) Curious to see if gulls really do follow the plough, I will spend an hour the following September standing in a muddy field above Dartmouth waiting to catch the moment. Things start quietly, but within minutes, as the number of birds increases, you can see how it might get quite unnerving.

Gulls following the plough

The path up to the Gribbin

Then we come out on a ledge, and in front of us is the beach. To the right there is a slatted bridge that leads on and up to the daymark. To the left there is a sort of causeway and a rusty winch.[6]

And there is the boat house. It is larger and better maintained than I had expected (I was about to say than it should be!). And that's the problem: whereas the beach is perfect, the boathouse is just too big – it's not supposed to be a holiday cottage that sleeps eight!

This is where Rebecca had her night-time trysts with Favell. This is where she arranged to meet him that last night to tell important news. This is where she taunted (in Max's version) her husband with the news of a child – an heir to Manderley that wasn't his. This is where she was murdered. It is now the ultimate holiday-let for the Daphne du Maurier fan.

Mrs de Winter talks of the unpredictable nature of the beach. She goes 'corridor-walking' and finds the west wing where Rebecca had her rooms. Not daring to enter, she looks out on the sea from an alcove window:

The Gribbin over banks of flowers

> *I looked out, and I saw below me the smooth grass lawns stretching to the sea, and the sea itself, bright green with white-tipped crests, whipped by a westerly wind and scudding from the shore.*

A moment later and the mood has changed,

The first view of the cove

The boathouse

A hurrying cloud hid the sun for a moment as I watched, and the sea changed colour instantly, becoming black, and the white crests with them very pitiless suddenly, and cruel, not the gay sparkling sea I had looked on first.

The excerpt quietly emphasizes the fragility of the relationship she finds herself in. It's a classic example of the way du Maurier endows almost every description she writes with subliminal references to the dramas that have, and will, take place, as she inexorably cranks up an unidentified sense of unease in her reader.

Today, however, the bay is bathed in bright sunshine. The air is warm, there is a little *Je Reviens*-type boat anchored out on the blue waters and one or two isolated sun-worshippers. This was Daphne du Maurier's favourite spot. She would sit on the beach doling out lemonade and sandwiches to her children, and no one would realise that she was a best-selling author.

There are wonderful photos of different generations of her and her family walking back up the hill above Happy Valley to Menabilly after long days on the beach. It was arriving at 5 in the morning and walking up past the lake at Pridmouth that she first explored Menabilly. This is the lake whose swans would inspire the short story *The Old Man*.

As usual, I manage to unearth a couple of curious facts. The main attraction listed in the Victorian guides, for example, was Dr Phillip Rashleigh's grotto just up behind the boathouse.

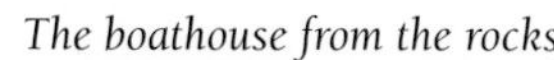

The boathouse from the rocks

Above: *Sun parasol*

Right: *The Gribbin seen from the beach*

He was a renowned geologist and his collection of minerals was the largest in the country. The grotto, whose doorway was made from the jawbone of a whale and whose inner walls were encrusted with crystals, pebbles, shells, fossils and ores, also vaunted – how times change – a beautiful asbestos roof hung with asbestos stalactites.

The other is that the lake during the war was illuminated, with false ships, quays and noises and served as a decoy for Fowey Harbour. The idea was to draw air attacks away from the real port which at that time was bristling with over 2000 US Navy personnel ready to leave on the word for the Normandy invasion. One imagines how, at the time, the tenants of Menabilly must have hoped for deadly accuracy on the part of the German bombers.

But where is the wreck? I cross over to the other side of the beach (or I should say to the other beach, apparently there are two, but this only becomes evident a high tide), in the direction of the Gribbin. I pass the pool sculpted in the rock by the Rashleigh family when sea-water bathing was all the rage.

I had seen a black and white photo of Daphne du Maurier sitting on a rock dwarfed by a piece of wreckage behind her. I had seen a later photo of Martyn Shallcross standing by a reduced fragment, clad all in red and *not* clutching, unusually, a frail and haunted looking du Maurier to his side.

The wreck has obviously rusted away even more since that time. I clamber over the slippery and viciously sharp rocks – and then, there it is. Two eyes like the hood of a cobra – the anchor shutes and the bowsprit fitting – rise up before me, jagged, twisted and so perfectly camouflaged with their surroundings as to be invisible from the beach. This, and a few other fragments, is all that is left of the *Romanie*, the ship that inspired one of the most famous scenes of modern British literature.

Rashleigh's bath

Fortunately for Captain Heip and his Belgian crew of eight, the services of the Fowey lifeboat were not required, the crew managing to clamber over the side of the vessel on to the rocks and reach dry land. And – small world – where were they were taken to recover from their ordeal before returning home? To the Seamens Christian Friend Society in Fore Street!

The bow of the Romanie

We make our way back up to the path. Looking back the wreck has disappeared once again. Polridmouth beach appeared in *Rebecca* and *Cousin Rachel* but some of the most memorable descriptions of it come in *The King's General*, written just after du Maurier had come to live at Menabilly.

The novel tells us that the cove had been used in the past for smuggling and was also the place where the silver collected by Jonathan Rashlegh was shipped out, to help the King's cause, via a secret passage that ran from the summer house in the grounds down to the beach.

More wreckage

The cove would later become the Dunkerque for the 5000-odd Parliamentarian foot-soldiers trapped on the headland (the 2000 horse managed miraculously to sneak out under cover of night right under the sleepy noses of the much embarrassed Royalists).

The cove is also the setting for perhaps the most poignant moment of the whole novel as Richard Grenville makes his escape.

Finally, du Maurier gives Honor Harris, towards the twilight of her life, a perfect description of the hushed beauty of this enchanting place at the ends of summer days,

> *Evenings of late summer, when the sun has set, and the moon has not yet risen, but the dew is heavy in the long grass.*
>
> *The sea is very white and still, without a breath upon it, and only a single thread of wash upon the covered Cannis rock. The jackdaws fly homeward to their nests in the warren. The sheep crop the short turf, before they too rub together beneath the stone wall by the winnowing place. Dusk comes slowly to the Gribbin hill, the woods turn black, and suddenly, with stealthy pad, a fox creeps from the trees in the thistle park, and stands watching me, his ears pricked.... Then his brush twitches and he is gone.*

A thin line of white over Cannis Rocks

CHAPTER 13

CASTLE DOR

I do a quick check on Amazon of the Daphne du Maurier Top 20. *Castle Dor* is languishing down in the bottom reaches of the chart along with *Julius, Gerald* and *The Golden Lads.* Margaret Forster's biography barely gives it a mention and even that is better than it has fared in some other works on the author. 'Neglected' is a word that will keep cropping up in this chapter.

Castle Dor, *1st GB edition, 1962*

It is probably because this retelling of the Tristan and Iseult myth set in nineteenth century Cornwall is not solely hers. The novel was started by Quiller-Couch in the 1920s but was left unfinished at his death – he had said that it would never be good enough to publish. In 1959, Q's daughter Foy happened upon the manuscript again and hit upon the idea of asking du Maurier to complete it. As du Maurier wrote in the *Sunday Telegraph* of April 1962, she took up the job, yes, with considerable trepidation, but above all "in memory of happy evenings long ago when Q was host at Sunday supper."

Maybe it is Q's style that has disenthused the reading public. The first part of the book is, to be fair, characterised by a slightly pedantic approach. There is a great deal of philology, etymology and a predilection for esoteric vocabulary. The meandering style with its overly-long sentence construction means that there is a considerable amount of rereading to make clear the relationships between the various parts of the narrative. The flow of the story stumbles.

Then at a certain point, the sentences become more incisive, the dialogue more vivid. Extraneous material of purely academic interest is pared down to a minimum and the pace of the story speeds up. Put very crudely, the pages are turning faster and the novel has started to grip you. Du Maurier has taken over.

Foy Quiller-couch wrote in the preface to the first edition in 1962 that du Maurier has "so cleverly woven her work into his, that I defy anyone to discover where the shuttle passed from his hand into hers". It thus becomes a challenge to try and work out where du Maurier starts and Q finishes. Not being able to 'cheat' and look at the manuscript in Exeter University library, I have made my own attempt to find the join. I may be totally wide of the mark but it is an interesting exercise.

Chapter 17, I remember, is the official hand-over point, but things are going on long before then. The wording of Foy's comment is important. She uses the phrase "woven her work into his" suggesting that it is not a seamless join that we are looking for but rather an intertwining of strands.

It seems to me that, here and there, there is 'a voice' more interested in topography than philology – a soldier's voice rather than an academic's. A voice which uses phrases that will almost appear verbatim in *Vanishing* and *Enchanted Cornwall*. The first comment perhaps is the unsuitability of Tintagel as a landing point for vessels "an impossibility if you look at the coast". Later, the widening of the perspective to consider Malpas on the Fal cannot fail to bring to mind Tommy Browning's beloved dish-mop lost one night during their honeymoon.

I also have the feeling that du Maurier would have left clues as to where her intervention was starting. It is tempting to think that the comment "it is a curious coincidence that no poet, or shall we call him investigator, has ever lived to conclude this particular story. His work has always been finished by another" was one such indication.

For me, because it is also accompanied by the changes in narrative technique outlined above, it is Chapter 12 'Comfort Me with Apples' that marks the real passing of the baton. Significantly "the cuckoo" is mentioned on no less than three occasions.

Then there are passages such as, "A train rattled over the viaduct above. 'That's the night express,' said Linnet. It stops at Plymouth: and after that one can fade off into another life and wake up in London." – that smack very much of du Maurier.

Finally, perhaps most interesting of all are the comments du Maurier makes in *Enchanted Cornwall*. She is at pains to underline the fact that Carfax is the one character who had her full sympathy, a Prospero-like figure who reminded her so much of Q himself. Similarly Carfax shares Q's great enthusiasm for his discoveries about the Tristan locations around Fowey.

She goes on to explain that it is he "who in some strange way sets in motion the whole story" and then quotes the prologue in its entirety. This prologue is, I think, du Maurier's work. It is typical of her 'beginnings' (see Chapter 15) and also serves the function of making Carfax the central character in the novel.

One phrase stands out from the rest "This most ancient cirque of Castle Dor, deserted, bramble-grown was the very nipple of a huge breast in pain, aching for discharge" Was she here gently mocking Q for the timid eroticism that had seeped into his prose in this emotionally super-charged story? It was Q, remember, who forbade his nephew ever to read *I'll Never be Young Again* or *Julius* because of their scurrilous content. Did Q really believe that the novel he had started was not up to his own high standards or did he perhaps deem its content unsuitable?

*****

The search for the places mentioned in the book starts off well enough. The Long Stone – the menhir – which originally marked the burial place of Tristan is impossible to miss as you drive into Fowey. It used to stand at Four Turnings outside the entrance to Menabilly. (It can be seen in its former location on page 130 of *Enchanted Cornwall*.)

Next on the agenda is Castle Dor itself. We drive past the first time without even realising. We turn the car round, and while I am studying the map trying to work out the location, I miss a 'grumpy-looking' (my wife's description) Dawn French who has pulled over to let us pass.

It's actually quite a dangerous place to visit. The road is quite heavily trafficked with speeding cars. As far as we can see, the only way to get in is for Rachel to stop, me to jump out and vault over the gate and her to pull off as quickly as possible so as not to get hit from behind. I will then phone her on the mobile when I have finished and she will drive down and hopefully be able to stop to pick me up.

A plaque tells that the site is 225 feet in diameter and was a village from the third to the first century BC. In the sixth century it surrounded the wooden hall of King Mark of Cornwall. On 31st August, 1644 it saw a battle in which the Parliamentarians were routed by the Royalists as recounted in *The King's General*.

The Long Stone, Tristan's burial place

Far left: *Inscription in front of the stone*

Left: *Plaque at Castle Dor*

Castle Dor from the air

Hawthorn on the ramparts

The site is formed by a circular rampart with an entrance surrounded by an oval-shaped earthwork which shielded the entrance to the first enclosure. I am glad that I had seen the aerial photos before coming. This would be very hard to make out at ground-level.

I clamber up into the centre of the circle. The grass is shin-deep and laden with dew and my shoes and trousers are soaked within minutes. Hawthorn and brambles make up the defences now – perhaps the remnants of some ancient palisade. One possible explanation for the site's name is that during the summer the walls were covered with yellow gorse flowers. Castle Dor would mean Golden Castle.

What is clear from up here though is the imposing location. It commands the whole of the countryside around. The panoramic views are due to its strategic positioning on the crest of the ridge that divides the river Fowey from Tywardreath and the sea and which runs down on to the Gribbin at the end of the promontory. Du Maurier's husband, with his "soldier's professional eye", was of the opinion that it could have been held against all-comers.

Looking towards St Austell

The site is, like the novel, neglected. The problem is that money is not forthcoming nor interest deep enough to support further excavations. It's a pity. As Bob Lewis, the affable and infectiously enthusiastic Tywardreath Player, points out to me, the site here and also that of the ancient priory in *The House on the Strand* are crying out for a visit from TV's archaeological Time Team.

After another hairy manoeuvre, we are off to find King Mark's private residence – Lancien, or Lantyan as the farm is known today. Foy Quiller-Couch recalls in her preface the day she rowed up the River Fowey with her father to Lantyan in search of Mark's Gate.

The road descends, transforming itself into a muddy track, and then there is the building in front of us. I take a photo from the car – an extremely zealous and protective farm-dog deters me from getting out for any other shots. The place is looking a bit run down, it has to be said – these farmers are certainly not getting rich on the back of the du Maurier-Tristan connection.

The view towards Tywardreath

Looking down towards the Fowey River

Above right: *The viaduct at Lantyan*

Below: *The farm at Lantyan*

I just can't find the lane that leads to the railway bridge below which Tristan fought but as we make our way towards Fowey I see the viaduct nestling in the valley and, risking life and limb once again, I manage to get a picture from the road.

Driving back to Fowey, I have the same feeling of disappointment that I experienced after my encounter with Dozmary Pool.

I have a good mind to ring Tony Robinson myself.

CHAPTER 14
TYWARDREATH & KILMARTH

Her beloved Tommy died in 1965. Just how great a blow this was she recounted in a moving piece entitled *Death and Widowhood* in *The Rebecca Notebook*. Shortly after, she realised that she would also soon have to leave Menabilly. Her way of dealing with all this was to write. She would collaborate on a project with her son, Kits – a non-fiction work called *Vanishing Cornwall*. It dealt with the history and disappearing traditions of the county and was a chance to reminisce over happy memories with her husband. It also looked forward to the threat posed to Cornwall by mass tourism – a theme she would take up again in *Rule Britannia*.

She had been offered by Phillip Rashleigh the dower house of Kilmarth, and although she would, with time, come to consider this as her home, she was, at the beginning, full of anger at the thought of having to give up Menabilly.

Kilmarth and the gates

Kilmarth

To a certain extent, it was understandable. She had discovered the house in a terrible state of neglect and spent over £30,000 in the 1940s renovating the roof. She basically saved the place. She pours out her feelings in her letters to Oriel Malet. Having read these, you can appreciate the immense significance packed into the one line caption in *Vanishing Cornwall* that accompanies the photo of 'her' house: "The Rashleighs own Menabilly".

Kilmarth from the turning to Polkerris

Nevertheless, she picked herself up and threw herself into the history of Kilmarth and the area, taking inspiration from, or perhaps refuge in, the past. As the facts and ideas started to ferment in her mind, a new novel was soon 'brewing'.

She discovered the house was built on fourteenth century foundations. The name Kilmarth means in Cornish 'Mark's retreat'. This all tied in with Castle Dor and the Tristan and Iseult legend. Nothing was surer to fire up her imagination than the last outpost of the famous king. A previous occupant, a Professor Singer, who used to conduct strange experiments involving bottled embryos in the cellar of the house, was the first, in fact, to suggest that Castle Dor should be excavated.

Poring over her ancient tithe map, however, what fascinated her even more was the priory that used to stand in the nearby town of Tywardreath. The priory had been under the protection and guidance of the great Benedictine monastery of St Sergius and Bacchus in Angers and was founded around 1088. It was in a fine position in the middle of fertile farmland and, at that time, close to the sea. The inlet at Par used to reach as far inland as the present-day church and the former priory, meaning that the long cargo ships of the time could run straight in and unload on the beach.

This is the landscape that Honor Harris looks out on at the opening of *The King's General,*

> *September, 1653. The last of summer. The first chill winds of autumn. The sun no longer strikes my eastern window as I wake, but, turning laggard, does not top the hill before eight o'clock. A white mist hides the bay until noon, and hangs about the marshes too, leaving, when it lifts, a breath of cold air behind it. Because of this, the tall grass in the meadow never dries, but long past midday shimmers and glistens in the sun, the great drops of moisture hanging motionless upon the stems.*

Although records tell us that at the time the Benedictine monasteries were the principal centres of art and education in England, they were also important business concerns. Running probably with a maximum of seven or eight monks, the job of the priory was to administer the lands and property of the Mother House. By the thirteenth century its possessions stretched over much of Devon and Cornwall. This meant income from tithes on tin, fish, wool, and lamb from as far afield as Totnes and Brixham in Devon.

There were clear economic and financial motives behind the extremely generous charter granted to the inhabitants of Fowey by the prior of Tywardreath in the first quarter of the thirteenth century. Fowey was prospering and it was in the priory's interest to keep on good terms with these powerful merchants. In addition, the old-fashioned long ship known as the

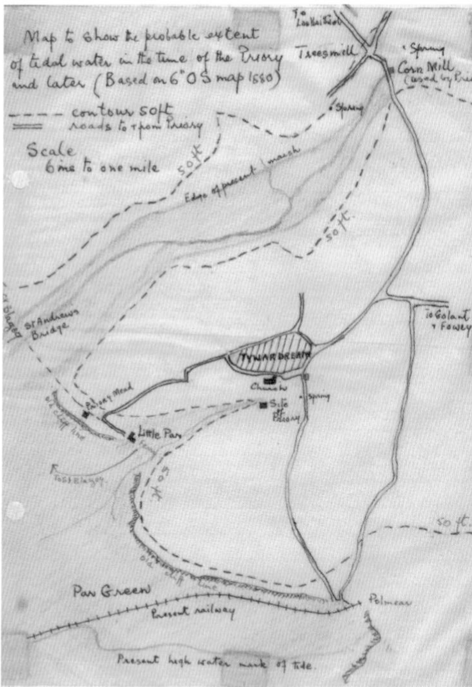

Tidal reach in medieval times

Tywardreath church

Tywardreath church, the tower

Tywardreath church from the east

knorr mentioned above was being replaced by the deeper draught vessels of the Baltic traders of the Hanseatic League – the cog. This is the ship depicted on so many medieval town seals including Dartmouth and Fowey. These craft with their much increased cargo capacity needed to unload in deep water at a quay, which was just what Fowey had in abundance. The priory would thus have access to these vessels if needed, and also continued to bank all the harbour dues from the town.

For the income came not only from tithes. There were also the dues and rents, not to mention the fines from the local courts that they managed.

The Cornish Archives are rich in documents from the period. Reading the rolls of the medieval Law Courts, you are quickly transported back to the world of *The Name of the Rose*. From the year 1446 we read;

> *Order to all having dung-heaps in the streets to remove them before next court, on penalty of 12d each.*
>
> *Inquiry whether Robert Keasse assaulted Joan, wife of Peran Busse (whose husband supports her), and took and held her while Rose, Robert's servant, struck her and beat her.*
>
> *Nicholas Elys drew blood from 1 monk with a knife, whence 2s 6d blodewite to the lord.*
>
> *Amercement of 40d for everyone who has a pig wandering within the borough without lord's grace*

Although none of the original buildings are still standing, we know that the priory itself stood to the south of today's churchyard, roughly on the site of the present-day Newhouse Farm. In fact, looking at Google Earth, a substantial rectangular outline, lying obliquely in relation to the present farm buildings, is visible precisely at this point.

In 1822 *The Gentleman's Magazine* reported that the then vicar had obtained leave to dig the ground on the supposed site in search of stones for erecting a vicarage.

He discovered that the priory chapel had been 80 feet long by 57 feet wide, with a semi-circular end towards the east, strengthened by four buttresses of wrought Pentewan stone and ornamented by four pilasters. All the carved work was executed, in his opinion, with much skill and taste.

Examples of this carved work are still visible: at the foot of the present-day church tower; in a specially prepared niche inside the church; above the door of Myrtle Cottage across the road from the church and incorporated into the walls of the Old Vicarage.

Above: *Remains of the old priory at the foot of the tower*

Left: *The location of the old priory*

The church itself houses memorials to the Rashleigh family and Honor Harris. There is also the black slate tombstone of the infamous Prior Collyns.

The patron saints of the priory, Sergius and Bacchus were interesting enough in themselves. They had been high-ranking officers in the Roman army, and were held very much in favour until exposed as secret Christians when they refused to enter a pagan temple.

It also seems that these "paired" saints were also a couple. The oldest Greek text of their martyrdom (Bacchus was flogged to death and Sergius beheaded after being paraded round the city in women's clothes) describes them as "erastai" or lovers. Their names pop up again in same-sex wedding rites of the

Above: *Fleur de Lys at the Old Vicarage*

Left: *Myrtle Cottage's Virgin and Child*

Above: *Carved stone from the priory*

Above middle: *Rashleigh memorial in the church*

Above right: *Plaque to Honor Harris*

Below: *The 'Virgin and Child' on Myrtle Cottage*

Eastern Orthodox Church between the fourth and nineth centuries AD. Further investigation throws up the following cryptic comments from a French website: "The questions of the distancing of the Abbey from the old city of Angers (800 metres) and the dedication, rare in the west, to Sergius, have yet to be answered" In fact the 'Virgin and Child' from the priory, now located above the front door to Myrtle Cottage opposite the church, does look suspiciously like the young Bacchus tightly clasping an older Sergius.

Judith Cook writes that du Maurier had discovered that older monks had encouraged pretty young men into joining the priory for homosexual orgies. She certainly incorporated the bawdy, dissolute behaviour of the brothers into the novel and uses it to heighten the tension, hinting at the ambiguity of the relationship between Dick (the narrator) and Magnus. On one of his 'trips' back in time Dick finds himself just outside the priory. He sees two monks in the muddy yard flicking at the bare buttocks of a young novice with flails. An onlooking horseman calls out to them, "Don't bleed him yet. The prior likes sucking-pig served without sauce"

On another occasion, the drug parachutes Magnus into the monks' sleeping quarters. Magnus tells Dick, much to the latter's amusement, that what he saw going on was exactly what you would suppose a bunch of medieval Frenchmen thrown together would get up to…

From the records in the Archives, it certainly seems that, possibly distracted by the great wealth they were administering, the handful of monks were losing sight of their original religious vocation. Although I could not discover the source of the comment in Fortescue Hitchin's *The History of Cornwall* (1824) that the Prior preferred to be paid in kind for the lands he rented out, and precisely "Concubinam tive nitidam puellam", the repeated admonitions from different Bishops to the Prior over the years show that things were clearly getting out of hand.

The first problems emerge in a letter from the Bishop in 1504:

> *Enjoining you and the monks to celebrate divine service according to the rules of your order, rigidly to observe the regular disciplines of your order, all to sleep in one dormitory in individual beds assigned to you and to dine in one refectory, not to leave the premises of the monastery without specific permission of the prior.*

In 1513, the situation has, if anything, deteriorated and the new Bishop Oldham reprehends them once again. They are not to frequent taverns or converse with women, at least those of suspect character, and on no account to admit them within the enclosure. These admonitions to be read four times a year in the Chapter House.

Eight years later, it is Bishop Veysey's turn to point out that now 'none of their vows' – divine service, obedience, or the silence of the cloister – are being observed. No brother was to leave the precincts without leave and then only with a companion; all windows and places by which women might enter or brothers go out were to be closed.

During most of this time a certain Prior Collyns was theoretically 'in charge'. He was a bibulous, corrupt, drunkard, incredibly obstinate yet somehow likeable old man whose character shines down to us across the centuries. The church was trying to get rid of him. His exchanges with the various Bishops make most amusing reading. It is probable that du Maurier based her Prior on this character even though the novel itself spans a period of time from 1320 to the Black Death in 1348.

With the Dissolution of the Monasteries in 1536, Tywardreath – whose not insubstantial income had gone somewhere but not into the priory coffers – was one of the first to go.

Not surprisingly, none of the five or six monks resident at the time of the suppression decided to continue in Holy Orders. The priory itself was plundered by the local townsfolk for its stone. The Prior's personal wood-panelled chamber was transferred to the Rashleighs' town house.

Our old friend, Prior Collyns, is still there at the end trying to ship some of the more valuable dressed Trewanten stone back to the mother house in France. The ship was unfortunately

Tower of the Bishop's Palace, Paignton. In The House on the Strand, *the Bishop writes to the Prior from here.*

Prior Collyns' tombstone

The Saltire Cross – the symbol of the priory

wrecked just off Polridmouth Bay and rumour is that much finished up at Menabilly. Later, in fact, on a walk around the Rashleigh estate, we come across a roundel bearing the carved saltire cross of the Priory Arms. The same cross with four fleur-de-lis now appears on the present church's flag.

*****

I remember reading the cover of *The House on the Strand* and being put off at first by the idea of time travel – I've never been a big fan of *Doctor Who*. It was weeks before I got round to starting reading – it all just sounded too far-fetched.

I was wrong. Du Maurier uses a technique similar to that of the *Scapegoat* and its double-theme where the reader is not even given time to doubt the unusual premise. With remarkable sleight of hand she needs just a page to take you from normal world to complete suspension of reality. What's more, you are well and truly hooked into the bargain.

The present church's banner

Likewise in *The House on the Strand* – from the first sentence you are back in time and you never question it.

When she describes the feelings of nausea and anxiety that accompany Dick's return to the present, she knows she can cleverly tap into the universal physical feelings of guilt familiar to anyone who has ever had to try to live a secret or a double life. Dick becomes increasingly absorbed by his trips back in time and, inevitably, his marriage suffers.

The book is a marvellous metaphor for her life of writing. She spent hours a day engrossed in her work and lost in the world of her imagination. Lost to the ones who loved her, too. There is a quote in Flavia Leng's biography to the effect that when she was writing:

> *She was in a world of her own where we were not welcome. Her need for space, for freedom, was greater than her need for us. We would lose sight of her, she would become that far-off figure in a "never never land", out of reach. She lived in distant times and places, peopled by the characters in her books, and they were beyond our childish comprehension.*
>
> *My father would shrug his shoulders and sigh, and he would remark to us, "Your mother lives in a dream".*

On another occasion, Tommy Browning would put it more bluntly: "Daphne would walk into a bloody lamp-post and not notice because she was so wrapped up in her writing"

Surely she was thinking as she wrote *The House on the Strand* of how much her husband and family must have suffered from these 'absences'; the pain she must have caused. An earlier collection of short stories, *The Apple Tree* (1952), had looked at the impact and the consequences of an individual's egoistical behaviour on the people around them. Now in this later novel she causes Dick's family life to disintegrate. A powerful wintry description highlights the bleakness and isolation of his situation and foreshadows the end,

> *It was bitter cold; not the swift, cutting blast that sweeps across high ground, but the dank chill of a valley where winter sunshine does not penetrate, nor cleansing wind. The silence was the more deadly, for the river rippled past me without sound, and the stunted willows and alder growing beside it looked like mutes with outstretched arms, grotesquely shapeless because of the burden of snow they bore upon their limbs. And all the while the soft flakes fell, descending from a pall of sky that merged with the white land beneath.*

His wife and children leave for America and he is left paralysed – presumably for life.

*****

The Apple Tree, *1st edition, 1952*

Critics have seen in du Maurier's male narrators her self-confessed inner male; her number two personality (as she calls it); the famous 'boy in the box'. Dick is lost in the past, searching for his ideal woman, Isolda, whom he can never attain. He can only stand by and watch as she makes love (Freud would have something to say regarding this 'primal scene' image). Would it be too much to say that in the novel, Dick's search for the ideal woman parallels that of the author for her mother?

So much has been said about Gerald that it almost hides the conspicuous absence of Muriel du Maurier. Her mother was certainly jealous of Daphne's extremely close relationship with her father. What's more du Maurier seems at times to have been almost in collusion with him over his various mistresses.

Gerald du Maurier gave his name to the famous cigarettes

In a sense the whole of her work had dealt with the theme of the absent mother. *The Loving Spirit* has an overarching virtual maternal archetype in Janet. We see the disastrous consequences of father-daughter incest in *Julius*. Mary Yellan leaves the peaceful maternal Helford for the fear and violence of the masculine world of *Jamaica Inn*.

Rebecca can be read in so many ways but at least one is to see the nameless Mrs de Winter as Daphne, Maxim as her father and Rebecca as her mother. In *Frenchman's Creek*, Dona has a romantic fling but, at the end of the day, being a mother is the most important thing. In *The King's General* one of the most touching aspects of the book is the surrogate maternal relationship which builds up between Honor and the boy. *The Scapegoat* has the moving scene where John patches up the relationship with Jean de Gues' mother and brings her not only back into family life but, literally, back to life.

In the final letter quoted in full in the Margaret Forster book, du Maurier talks of the terrific reliance and love she had had for Ferdie. She also writes that Ellen Doubleday was the mother she had never had. *September Tide* which dealt with her relationship with Ellen was originally called *Mother* – after the change of title it still retained the dedication, 'To my Mother'. She even told Ellen that she still had dreams about killing her mother. Finally, Ellen was also the inspiration for *My Cousin Rachel* – a tale of two men lacking a mother figure, one of whom ends up killing the very object of his desire.

Du Maurier greatly admired the work of Carl Gustave Jung. She would undoubtedly have come across this passage from his most famous work *The Archetypes and the Collective Unconscious*. The type of woman he describes in the following passage has what he terms a negative mother-complex.

> *All instinctive processes meet with unexpected difficulties; either sexuality does not function properly, or the children are unwanted, or maternal duties seem unbearable, or the demands of marital life are responded to with impatience and irritation.*
>
> *Again resistance to the mother can sometimes result in a spontaneous development of intellect for the purpose of creating a sphere of interest in which the mother has no place. Intellectual development is often accompanied by the emergence of masculine traits in general.*

Tregaminion Church

It certainly is a thought-provoking paragraph.

*****

We leave Tywardreath and make our way back down to the main road. The hill out of Par is a chance to put your foot down, just as du Maurier used to in her little red Daf.

She said at one point – I think it was after a trip abroad that she hadn't particularly enjoyed – that from then on she had no desire to go further east than Looe or further west than Falmouth. It's true: Du Maurier Country, especially from the 1940s onwards was concentrated in a very small area. As we pass the gates to Kilmarth, it is only a matter of yards before we come to Tregaminion church (where the memorial service was held) and then less than a stone's throw to the gates of Menabilly's west lodge.

Talking of Menabilly, it is coming up to 3 o'clock and I have an appointment… with Sir Richard Rashleigh.

CHAPTER 15
MENABILLY

Each of the two gateposts at the entrance to Menabilly sports a 'Strictly Private' sign. Another further ahead reads 'Beware of the Bull'.

I judge it prudent to check before proceeding. I ring the bell of the gatehouse. A smiling gentleman answers the door. "We have to pick up the key for the Gamekeeper's Cottage", I explain. "You'll be looking for Sir Richard", he replies, "just carry straight on down to the house."

Sir Richard Rashleigh. It had seemed strange to see his name there at the bottom of the email all those months ago. When I explained I was working on a book about Daphne du Maurier, he told me how a long time back the family had held a pow-wow and decided on a blanket 'No' to anyone requesting interviews about the writer. I could take photos of the cottage – that was in the public domain on the website anyway, and he had no objections to shots of the odd rhododendron or two – but absolutely none of the main house.

The Gate House, Menabilly

The drive crosses an open paddock dotted with trees and the occasional pheasant. Two rusted white gates stand open. You can see the gravelled space in front of the house now.

The first impression is that it is smaller than I had imagined. But there is no disappointment - the house is a little jewel. The stone is the most delicate shade of grey, and the building is perfectly geometric, at least from this angle. Built on two floors, the façade comprises two rows of seven, mullioned windows. The central section of three stands slightly proud of the two lateral sections.

What strikes you next is the front door. The bottom section, of very dark wood, is elaborately carved, vaguely medieval, a relic of a ship perhaps or from the priory? The door is flanked by two columns and surmounted by a modest, square, carved stone coat of arms of the Rashleigh family.

Gamekeeper's Cottage

Through the glass of the door, I can see someone advancing towards me, accompanied by two barking dogs – a large black labrador and a black and white spaniel. For a split second, I am concentrating on whether I will have to fend off the two hounds and forget to look through into the hallway. A moment later, the door is closed, the dogs are playing on the drive, and Sir Richard is standing in front of me, keys in hand. He is dressed in a check shirt, grey pullover and green cords. Very friendly, but no handshake. I remind him of who I am and he reminds me of what we have agreed.

The track leads off down through the forest. We gingerly negotiate the many pot-holes left after the recent heavy rains. The road forks either side of a pond and to the left the Gamekeeper's Cottage is standing on top of a small grassy hill.

It is nicely laid out inside. Downstairs there is a spacious kitchen-dining room and a lounge with a real fire and bookcase of some forty or so novels (not one du Maurier). Upstairs there are three bedrooms. It is clean, simple, and thanks to the Rayburn stove, wonderfully warm. A real little Hansel and Gretel-style cottage.

But it is the location which is most impressive. Behind, a hill covered in daffodils and primroses rises to the woods. In front of and around the cottage runs a stream and across the stream it's

The cottage from the stream

Above left: *The forest around the cottage*

Above: *Giant trees*

trees, trees and more trees. Some are fallen and covered in moss, others are contorted and twisted, still others, draped with gigantic creepers, tower into the clouds – and this as far as the eye can see.

Once unpacked, we decide to follow the sound of the breakers to the beach. The track leads on past the pond and high up above the stream. This is the Happy Valley so often mentioned in *Rebecca*. It is the end of March and the trees are still bare after the cold winter. The rhododendrons and azaleas are in bud but there is no trace of a bloom. The charms of Menabilly are proving elusive.

We can hear now the waves crashing on the shingle. Down at the beach the wind is biting. I try to climb up towards the Gribbin but the week's downpours have rendered the path a quagmire and I turn back. Cold, wet and (yours truly) covered in mud, we return to the welcome warmth of the cottage.

A couple of hot cups of tea later, I decide to explore the hill at the back of the house. A steep path leads up through a corridor of yellow flowers. The terrain opens out into scrubby woodland carpeted with wild garlic. Then off to the left I see it. It looks like a bulkier version of the monolith in *2001 – A Space Odyssey*, and just as incongruous in this setting. Standing there amongst the trees is a massive block of smooth polished granite with a topknot of a Rashleigh coat of arms perched aloft as a bit of an afterthought. The inscription tells of the

Polridmouth Cove

explorations of a Rashleigh (it proves to be William), in the early 1800s. This rings a bell. Back down in the cottage I check my copy of *My Cousin Rachel*.

> *topping the woods, before plunging to descent and the keeper's cottage in the gulley, Ambrose had set up a piece of granite… Upon the slab of granite he had scrolled some mention of the lands where he had travelled, and a line of doggerel at the end to make us laugh when we looked at it together.*

This is where Phillip read the fateful letter from Ambrose that turned up after his death and which would have such a bearing on subsequent events. He digs a hole for the letter beneath the slab and walks back down past the cottage. Later, as we know, he will reread the letter at a crucial moment of the story.

I am feeling quite pleased with myself. I have not seen a photo of the block of granite in any publication, nor, for that matter, any mention of it.

I sit down and idly flick through the guest book. One couple have stayed an astonishing eleven times and thank Richard and Emma Rashleigh for the bottle of bubbly left to toast their 40th

The boathouse approaching from Happy Valley

The cove in March

The Rashleigh coat of arms and the monolith

wedding anniversary. The early part of the book, however, reveals that previous visitors have an almost Kit Williams-like obsession with treasure hunts in the woods and annoyingly all feature the monolith as a clue. Fortunately, none mention the connection with *My Cousin Rachel.* My discovery is still safe.

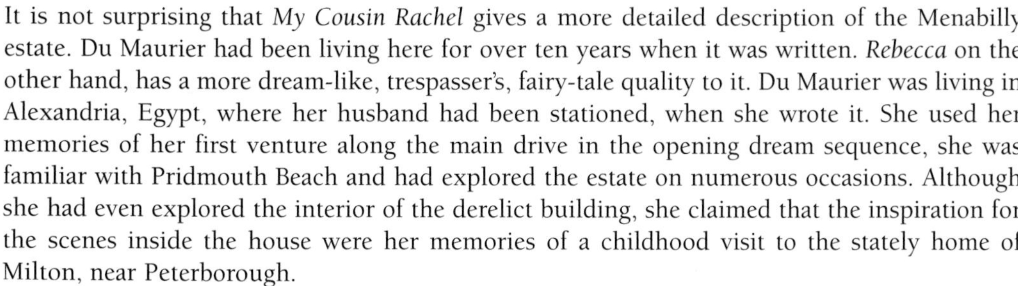

It is not surprising that *My Cousin Rachel* gives a more detailed description of the Menabilly estate. Du Maurier had been living here for over ten years when it was written. *Rebecca* on the other hand, has a more dream-like, trespasser's, fairy-tale quality to it. Du Maurier was living in Alexandria, Egypt, where her husband had been stationed, when she wrote it. She used her memories of her first venture along the main drive in the opening dream sequence, she was familiar with Pridmouth Beach and had explored the estate on numerous occasions. Although she had even explored the interior of the derelict building, she claimed that the inspiration for the scenes inside the house were her memories of a childhood visit to the stately home of Milton, near Peterborough.

*****

We have heard talk of deer in the forest. Betsy, the smallest, wants to go and search. We walk back down the Happy Valley, double back on ourselves and climb a ramson-carpeted trail up the hill. Then through a V formed by two silver birch trunks three brown-eyed faces are looking towards us. Our gazes meet for a few seconds and in an instant they are off, delicately springing through the undergrowth, their white rumps bobbing up and down. We veer off the path in an attempt to get closer. The wood flattens out into a wonderful daffodil-planted glade. Of the deer

Looking for deer

there is no sign, but above a mossy ridge chimneys are visible. We have unknowingly strayed backed towards Menabilly. What I had read in *Rebecca*, and heard said on many occasions, immediately becomes clear: it does lie as if in a cupped hand, becoming visible only at the last moment if you approach from the south as we have done. This clearly was important for safety at a time when the chief threats came from the sea.

I have a strong sensation that I am trespassing and so we make our way back to the track and the cottage.

Later, when night has fallen, I step out onto our little lawn. The only sounds are the owls hooting, the stream as it runs down towards the sea and the waves breaking down at Pridmouth Cove. The gnarled bare branches of the tree in front reach out like a thousand ghoulish fingers towards the full moon which disappears and reappears as the clouds scud across the black sky.

*****

I lie in bed but cannot sleep. Too many thoughts are crowding into my head.

I think it was Quiller-Couch who said that Daphne du Maurier would live to rue the day that *Rebecca* became so successful. She would be branded from then on with the ultimate taboo-word in literature, 'popular'. She, herself, wrote despairingly on numerous occasions, "I fear I will never be considered a great writer".

The reason why *Rebecca* sold so well was because it had something for everyone. Not only does it deal with themes of universal appeal which reached out to an enormous readership, but also, because most of the novel takes place inside the narrator's head, it lends itself to a variety of "readings" of the triangle, Rebecca, Maxim and Mrs de Winter.

The debate then starts as to whether it is based on du Maurier's jealousy of Jan Ricardo, Browning's previous liaison. Or, perhaps, Rebecca and Mrs De Winter are the two facets of du Maurier's personality that we have touched on before. Or is it something deeper – is Rebecca the mother figure, and Max the father figure for the young Daphne?[7]

Yet, the fact is that, for the myth to have continued, despite this multiplicity of interpretations that can be brought to the novel, the majority of readers must have read *Rebecca* simply as a straightforward love-story. Du Maurier herself was at pains to point out that it was a "study in jealousy" – a minute examination of the details of this all-consuming passion - if anything the opposite of a 'romance'. Notwithstanding this, and due in part to her following up *Rebecca* with *Frenchman's Creek,* she was awarded, as a writer, the epithet 'romantic' and to a large extent it has stuck ever since.

It is the novels with female narrators that fare worst, susceptible as they are to this less-critical, less-reflective approach, laying themselves open to more or less superficial readings. Although this was commercially advantageous, I doubt very much that du Maurier knowingly played on this as has been suggested. In fact, the indications are that she found it extremely frustrating from a personal point of view as a writer.

What aggravated matters even more was that the literary critics reviewing her novels were usually males who often read what they expected to read from a female author.

Finally, as we look around to see who else we can blame for this remarkable critical neglect, we come to the films - those Hollywood blockbusters which were, for many, their only experience of du Maurier. Hitchcock, it has to be said, made somewhat of an art, intentionally or not, of emasculating du Maurier's work. *Rebecca* the film has very little of the deep-rooted jealous anxiety of *Rebecca* the novel and the uneasy feeling of the later stages is completely lost when there is no longer a question of murder. *Jamaica Inn,* similarly, is far less sinister without the vicar, Francis Davey, in control. Hitchcock, of course, could, when necessary, conveniently pass the buck on to the Hays Office, the American censor at the time.

A 1947 Chilean edition in Spanish of La Sucesora, *the novel that led to the* Rebecca *plagiarism trial*

So, thanks to film directors, reviewers and readers – all lacking in critical awareness and possessed of standard stereotypical sexist 'romantic' expectations, we arrive at the bizarre situation in which, for example, the magazine *Woman's Own* could publish in 1953 a vicious little short story like *The Little Photographer* with the two-page spread seen in the illustration. Bizarre, because this subversive little gem is embedded in page after page of the most excruciatingly sexist views regarding women. Just one example:

> *He says: "I've never seen this shirt washed so white before! How did you manage it?*
> *She says: Oxydol, darling! And it's not only your shirt. It's all my white things. I'm really proud of them.*

Even today the repercussions continue. Most people still find it difficult to believe that Daphne du Maurier could have possibly been the author of such chilling short stories as *The Birds* and *Don't Look Now*. Of works such as *The House on the Strand* and the *Scapegoat*, the majority of casual readers remain blissfully unaware.

*****

And yet, there is, of course, so much more to du Maurier than the merely 'popular' or 'romantic'.

As a teller of stories, as a writer who knows how to maintain suspense, who keeps the pages turning, not letting you put the book down, she is up there with the greats.

She was arrogant, bored and beautiful – to her a man's love and life were small prices to pay for her own amusement

The Little Photographer

Beginning a brilliant three-part serial
BY DAPHNE DU MAURIER

THE Marquise lay on her chaise longue on the balcony of the hotel. She wore only a wrapper, and her sleek gold hair, newly set in pins, was bound close to her head in a turquoise bandeau that matched her eyes. Beside her chair stood a little table, and on it were three bottles of nail varnish all of different shades.

She had dabbed a touch of colour on to three separate finger-nails, and now she held her hand in front of her to see the effect. No, the varnish on the thumb was too red, too vivid, giving a heated look to her slim olive hand, almost as if a spot of blood had fallen there from a fresh-cut wound.

The middle finger was touched with a sheen of silk neither crimson nor vermilion, but somehow softer, subtler; the sheen of a peony in bud, not yet opened to the heat of the day but with the dew of the morning upon it still. A peony, cool and close, looking down upon lush grass from some terraced border, and later, at high noon, the petals unfolding to the sun.

Yes, that was the colour. She reached for cotton-wool and wiped away the offending varnish from her other finger-nails and then slowly, carefully, she dipped the little brush into the chosen varnish, and, like an artist, worked with swift, deft strokes.

When she had finished she leant back in her chaise longue, exhausted, waving her hands before her in the air to let the varnish harden—a strange gesture, like that of a priestess. She looked down at her toes, appearing from her sandals, and decided that presently, in a few moments, she would paint them too; olive hands, olive feet, subdued and quiet, surprised into sudden life.

Not yet, though. She must rest, relax. It was too hot to move from the supporting back of the chaise longue and lean forward, crouching, eastern fashion, for the adorning of her feet. There was plenty of time.

Time, in fact, stretched before her in an unwinding pattern through the whole long, languorous day.

She closed her eyes.

The distant sound of hotel life came to her as in a dream, and the sounds were hazy, pleasant, because she was part of that life yet free as well, bound no longer to the tyranny of home.

A guest ordered coffee on the terrace below. The smoke of his cigar came floating upwards to the balcony. The Marquise sighed, and her lovely hands drooped down like lilies on either side of the chaise longue.

This was peace, this was contentment. If she could hold the moment thus for one more hour . . . But something warned her, when the hour was past, the old demon of dissatisfaction, of tedium, would return, even here where she was free at last, on holiday.

A bumble-bee flew on to the balcony, hovered over the bottle of nail varnish and entered the open flower, picked by one of the children, lying beside it. His humming ceased when he was inside the flower. The Marquise opened her eyes and saw the bee crawl forth, intoxicated. Then dizzily once more he took the air and hummed his way. The spell was broken.

The Marquise picked up the letter from Edouard, her husband, that had fallen on to the floor of the balcony.

". . . And so, my dearest, I find it impossible to get to you and the children after all. There is so much business to attend to, here at home, and you know I can rely on no one but myself. I shall, of course, make every effort to come and fetch you at the end of the month. Meanwhile, enjoy yourself. I know the sea air will do you good . . ."

The Marquise let the letter fall back again on to the balcony floor. The little droop at the corner of her mouth, the one tell-tale sign that spoilt the smooth lovely face, intensified. It had happened again. Always his work. The estate, the farms, the forests, the business men that he must see, the sudden journeys that he must take, so that in spite of his devotion for her he had no time to spare.

BEFORE her marriage, they had told her how it would be. "C'est un homme très sérieux, Monsieur le Marquis, vous comprenez." How little she had minded, how gladly she had agreed, for what could be better in life than a Marquis who was also "un homme sérieux"?

What more lovely than that château and those vast estates? What more imposing than the house in Paris, the retinue of servants, humble, bowing, calling her Madame la Marquise?

A fairy-tale world to someone like herself, brought up in Lyons, the daughter of a hard-working surgeon, an ailing mother. But for the sudden arrival of Monsieur le Marquis she might have found herself married to her father's young assistant, and that same day-by-day in Lyons continuing forever.

A romantic match, surely. Frowned on at first by his relatives, most certainly. But Monsieur le Marquis, homme sérieux, was past forty. He knew his own mind. And she was beautiful. There was no further argument. They married. They had two little girls. They were happy. Yet sometimes . . .

The Marquise rose from the chaise longue and, going into the bedroom, sat down before the dressing-table and removed the pins from her hair. Even this effort exhausted her. She threw off her wrapper and sat naked before her mirror. Sometimes she found herself regretting that day-by-day in Lyons.

SHE remembered the laughter, the joking with other girls, the stifled giggles when a passing man looked at them in the street, the confidences, the exchange of letters.

Now, as Madame la Marquise, she had no one with whom to share confidences, laughter. Everyone about her was middle-aged, dull, rooted to a life long-lived that never changed. Those interminable visits of Edouard's relatives to the château. His mother, his sisters, his brothers, his sisters-in-law.

In the winter, in Paris, it was just the same. Never a new face, never the arrival of a stranger.

The only excitement was the appearance, perhaps, to luncheon of one of Edouard's business friends, who, surprised at her beauty when she entered the salon, flickered a daring glance of admiration, then bowed, and kissed her hand.

Watching such a one, during luncheon, she would make a fantasy to herself of how they would meet in secret, how a taxi would take her to his apartment, and leaving a small, dark ascenseur she would ring a bell and vanish into a strange unknown room.

But, the long luncheon over, the business friend would bow and go his way. And afterwards, she would think to herself, he was not even passably good-looking; even his teeth were false. But the glance of admiration, swiftly suppressed—she wanted that.

Now she combed her hair before the mirror, and parting it on one side tried a new effect; a ribbon, the colour of her finger-nails, threaded through the gold. Yes, yes . . .

And the white frock, later, and that chiffon scarf, thrown carelessly over the shoulders, so that when she went out on to the terrace, followed by the children and the English governess, and

[Continued overleaf

She demanded adulation as a woman's right

ILLUSTRATED BY AUBREY RIX

8 9

Woman's Own *Magazine*, *November 13th 1953*

When it comes to her descriptions of Cornwall (of which my favourites are sprinkled throughout this book) she has few peers.

Then there are her masterful closing scenes. Two recurrent themes in her work are, on the one hand, a desire to rebel and give expression to a more authentic-feeling inner self and, on the other, an opposing, deep need for emotional security. The interweaving of these two skeins leads to a tension which, left unresolved in the final pages of the novels, produces the hall-mark, ambiguous du Maurier ending.[8]

There are no easy denouements which untangle, or resolve, the conflicting positions – more often than not there is just a return to varying degrees of precarious domesticity. One thinks of *Jamaica Inn* and Mary Yellan riding off towards the Tamar with her horse-thief groom, Jem Merlyn; of *Frenchman's Creek* where Dona returns (but is it definitively?) to her unloved husband; and of course, most famous of all, *Rebecca*, whose open-ended climax, or lack of climax, has engendered so many sequels, so many what-might-have-happened-nexts, in the past few years.

'Sequels' ironically were what du Maurier liked least. For her, the contradictions of life had to be lived out to the full, it was part of the process of self-realization. There could be no coming down on one side or the other, no resolution, no happy, final 'conclusion' to the story.

My Cousin Rachel caught me unawares. Hot from my reading of Agatha Christie, I spotted all too quickly the laburnum tree in the Italian courtyard and soon had the mystery all sewn up in my mind. But, then du Maurier starts to sow the nagging doubt that Phillip, the first person narrator, might be far less reliable than he thinks he is. At the end, we simply do not know what actually happened. When the author was asked if Rachel was good or evil, she replied, "I don't know. You see, I was Phillip when I wrote the book".

It is in the later novels – *The Scapegoat* and *The House on the Strand* that she finds her true voice and total mastery of her craft. Revealingly, her voice is *his* voice – for both stories are told by male narrators. This mastery has come hand in hand perhaps with a greater understanding of her inner self. In *The House on the Strand*, written after her husband had died, the main character, significantly, finds himself at the end in an inconclusive place but with the door leading back to some sort of family security now definitively closed.

Her 'beginnings', too, have perhaps an even more masterful touch. By plunging straight into the thick of things, be they memories, dreams or ongoing situations, she provokes in her reader, (unfailingly in my case), a sensory-factual overload. With so many details cramming in, details that are as yet unclear and unfamiliar, as is their inter-relationship and the significance that they will subsequently have in the text, du Maurier creates those feelings of confusion, bewilderment and anxiety that the novel will go on to explain to some extent but never completely resolve.[8]

Fine examples of her 'opening technique' are *My Cousin Rachel, The King's General, Castle Dor* and *The House on the Strand.* And of course, once again, there is *Rebecca* whose opening dream sequence is as densely populated with disturbing sights, thoughts and images as a canvas by Hieronymus Bosch.

*****

Freddy

We are wakened each morning by Freddy. He stands proudly on his drain cover off to the left and at regular intervals reaches up on tip-toe, cawks loudly then beats his wings noisily, either in an attempt to ward off rival males or just to impress Mrs Pheasant who is busying about lower down near the stream.

Today we are up early. I want to find the original carriage drive that led from the lodge at Four Turnings the several miles to the main house – the drive that is described in those famous opening pages of *Rebecca*.

Early morning frost

We have found the drive

My plan is to follow a path that skirts the fields up behind the cottage – this should then intersect with the drive which we can then follow back down the valley. Easier said than done, as they say. I soon realise that the description in *Growing Pains* of Daphne and Angela's first attempt to follow the drive to the house was no over-exaggeration and that the nightmarish opening of *Rebecca* was, in fact, firmly rooted in reality.

The path is almost impossible to follow. Holly, brambles, fallen trees and sprawling rhododendrons bar the way. We are continually leaving the track and scrambling through dense undergrowth in an attempt to get round the obstacles. I have a map with me – a machete would have been more useful. After about an hour, I decide it is time to descend towards the stream. Intrepidly I go to scout ahead. When I get to the point where one leg is momentarily, worryingly, stuck fast in shin-deep black mud, I decide we have taken a wrong turning.

At this point, morale in the group is, to put it mildly, low. I manage to gain approval for one last attempt to find the drive. As Rachel constructively points out, we are completely lost anyway so what difference can it make.

Then down near the edge of the stream is a line of daffodils. Next, what looks like the border of a path. Further ahead, you can see where the solid rock has been cut to allow the passage of the drive. Though the way, at this point, is relatively unencumbered (someone has cut the giant trunks lying across the path) the landscape we are passing through is totally overgrown and out of control. Beeches, birches, firs, sequoias and monkey puzzles have grown 40, 50 perhaps 60 metres high. Fallen trunks are strewn in all directions. The central stream area has opened out and is filled with massive thickets of bamboo. And everywhere, the parasites are eating all they find, alive or dead. Ivy rising tens of metres is slowing choking the tallest trees. Fungi and ferns are growing out of the living branches. In places, a strange, spindly, silver-green, moss covers everything. A full-sized tree is growing straight out of a fallen log. A strange tumour-like growth the size of a small chest of drawers bursts from halfway up the trunk of a towering giant.

A monkey puzzle tree 50 metres high

The drive crosses the stream. Over on the other side of the swamp the first red rhododendrons come into sight. Not many, (the plant itself, however, is huge and will be truly spectacular when in full bloom), but the first we have seen.

Finally, after walking for almost three hours, the Keeper's Cottage appears through the trees on the opposite bank. Now it is just across the stream. It's then that the drive decides to lose itself completely in the tangle of undergrowth. It is too far to go back – the only way is to try and get across. Fortunately, there is a fallen tree which we can use as a bridge. A slightly boggy stretch; the stream; and we emerge unscathed with nothing more than wet feet. It's been the sort of adventure I haven't had since I was a teenager.

*****

Everything is covered in moss

Above left: *The stream*

Above middle: *A bridge over the stream*

Above right: *The Gamekeeper's Cottage appears on the opposite bank*

That afternoon we call into Fowey for provisions and I pop in to say hello to Ann at Bookends. I tell her that we found the drive. She asks how we are enjoying the cottage and if I have found the piece of granite yet. I tell her for the umpteenth time that she should really being writing this book, not me! She also (infuriatingly) just drops into the conversation that the two psychic old ladies in *Don't Look Now* were inspired by previous occupants of the cottage during du Maurier's time at Menabilly. I will check that one out, but I already know she is right.

That afternoon, we make our way down to Pridmouth again – new guests have moved into the cottage on the beach. Instead of retracing our steps we take another path back which runs up behind the beach house and up along the ridge above Happy Valley. Rachel is somewhat concerned that on the map it is marked as Hooker's Grove.

There are fields to the left, the stream valley to the right. Then the path turns to run alongside the top boundary of the field. The Gribbin is there on the headland. This is where the photos were taken of Daphne and her family walking up the hill after long summer days on the beach. We turn round and there is Menabilly. You can see now the flaming rhododendrons to the east and in front of the house that are just beginning to come into bloom. Some of them are truly enormous - in a couple of months the garden will be absolutely ablaze with crimson flowers.[10] One can imagine Margot Fonteyn taking archery lessons here with Tommy Browning in preparation for a forthcoming ballet. Or the Queen and Prince Phillip having afternoon tea and scones on the lawn.

With the house in front of us again, the feeling of intruding returns. Remembering my promise, I suppress the desire to take a lovely shot of the house through the banks of flowers. We walk back down to the cottage. The track takes us alongside the outhouses and curves around the back of the buildings. You can see where the ill-fated North Wing once stood. The back wall of

Left: *The fields above Polridmouth*

Below: *A huge rhododendron tree*

the house has nothing of the geometric elegance of the front. Corridors that obviously once lead to the vanished wing have been bricked up and the whole thing has the appearance of a large irregular French-style farmhouse-chateau.

That evening we decide on Sam's on the Beach in Polkerris for dinner. As we drive up past the house a high-ceilinged room at the side is illuminated by chandeliers.

The turning down to the cove is just before you get to Kilmarth. As we reach the foot of the hill, the sun drops behind a bank of clouds and, to use du Maurier's expression, we see 'The Spirit moving upon the Waters'.

The restaurant is housed in what was the old lifeboat station. Reading the plaques listing the rescues made by the lifeboats (named after members of the Rashleigh family) during the 1800s it becomes clear that this building was also a Rashleigh project. Rashleighs also built the small harbour we can see through the glass wall of the restaurant. The pub next door is the Rashleigh Inn. If you lived here on the Gribbin peninsula you were almost certainly an employee, a tenant of the family or a Rashleigh. They really were Lord and Masters of all they could see.

A magnificent scarlet bloom

Later, I sit in front of a wood fire, reading *Don't Look Now*. I remember du Maurier telling Oriel Malet how she had found Miss Wilcox one winter's day huddled downstairs in the freezing cold almost sightless due to a stroke. The description in the short story "middle sixties, masculine shirt with collar and tie, sports jacket, grey tweed skirt coming to mid-calf. Grey stockings and laced black shoes." certainly matches the description given by Flavia Leng of the two old ladies that lived at Southcott (as the cottage was originally called). Above all, in the novel and in real life, we have the "mystical-looking blue eyes".

Sam's Place. Polkerris

The next day is regrettably our last. Before dinner, I drive down into Par to get a bottle of wine to celebrate. As I cross the park towards the lodge, I start to wonder what it must be like to actually live here, in what is a truly different world to the one inhabited by mere common folk like you and me. What would it be like to exchange places with Sir Richard Rashleigh? A thought – is that how the novel, *The Scapegoat*, came into being? Was du Maurier wondering what it would be like to really own Menabilly?

A car – the new guests down at the beach house – enters the lodge gates and spotting me, stops most deferentially and pulls over onto the grass to let me pass. I am greeted by beaming smiles as I nonchalantly drive past. Maybe just for a moment I have been mistaken for one of the Lords of the Manor…

Dinner over, we take one final walk in the gathering dusk. Down to the beach and then up in front of the house and round. The light is fading as we reach the top of the hill. The cattle are huddled together in the twilight. A young bullock full of bravado makes a mock charge at us.

Off in the distance, there is a light on the buoy marking the Cannis rocks.

Just a couple of the windows of the house are illuminated.

There are whoops and hoots as children bounce on a trampoline off to the right, then excited shouting as they chase each other round to the back of the house. It's a family home. You can understand why the family might resent the du Maurier connection.

Du Maurier was fascinated by the characters from the past that peopled the house. The Rashleighs now find themselves in turn haunted by Daphne du Maurier, *The King's General*, *My Cousin Rachel*, and, of course, *Rebecca*.

*****

So there it is, my journey is at an end.

Reading du Maurier and visiting the places that she loved and which inspired her has been a stimulating experience. It has reawakened by interest in English history and the English countryside. She has rekindled my interest, dormant since university days, in Jung. I have discovered Charles Trenet. More importantly I have discovered a whole series of superb novels that I never knew even existed. Finally, I have discovered a beautiful part of Cornwall, and a selection of very different but all very charming, friendly people who are all very passionate about du Maurier, Cornwall and Cornish history.

Regrets?

I never did get to climb the Gribbin and my passage up to the pool at Frenchman's Creek was blocked by the fallen tree. Kilmarth and Ferryside were definitely off limits, but that I expected. And no, Sir Richard didn't in the end say to me, "Hello Bret, how was the journey? Why don't you come in for a glass of wine and I'll show you round"

But then when you think about it, it is right that it was so. Take Menabilly – we each have our own Menabilly inside our heads, the Menabilly of our imagination. To have seen inside would have destroyed that, just as seeing the 'boathouse' at Pridmouth Cove destroyed for ever 'my' boathouse that I had built up in my mind.

It is right that some things remain beyond the realm of our experience. There should be places that we travel to only in our imagination. We need some mystery.

In the Western world, it seems sometimes that we are obsessed with banishing all that is inexplicable, unfamiliar or irrational from our lives. We have come as a culture to analyse, dissect and ultimately destroy everything in an attempt to 'understand'.

We have lost our sense of awe and wonder when faced with our environment. We no longer have that religious reverence that our distant ancestors felt as they walked through their world.

The Spirit on the Waters, Polkerris

Instead we sit at home and smugly appropriate nature's astounding intricacies and design through the cosy medium of TV. Yet, at the very same time, we smother our planet with concrete and choke its atmosphere with our waste.

We no longer recognise the old symbols; the ancient myths have ceased to guide us. This is the moment when the unconscious, as Jung said, becomes so vital – it has become a question of spiritual being or non-being. Our sterile lives crave secrets and mystery. Our hearts cry out for deeper meaning.

That is just what Daphne du Maurier can give us.

> *The flowers that died would bloom again another year, the same birds build their nests, the same trees blossom. The old quiet moss smell would linger in the air, and bees would come, and crickets, and herons build their nests in the deep dark woods. The butterflies would dance their merry jig across the lawns, and spiders spin foggy webs, and small startled rabbits who had no business to come trespassing poke their faces through the crowded shrubs. There would be lilac and honeysuckle still, and the white magnolia buds unfolding slow and tight beneath the dining-room window. No one would ever hurt Manderley. It would lie always in a hollow like an enchanted thing, guarded by the woods, safe, secure, while the sea broke and ran and came in again in the little shingle bays below.*

DAPHNE DU MAURIER'S LIFE

Daphne du Maurier was born in London on 12 May, 1907. She came from a highly artistic background. Her grandfather, George, was the author of the novels *Trilby* and *Peter Ibbetson*. Her mother, Muriel, and father, Gerald, were both actors. Sir Gerald du Maurier was famous above all for his portrayal of Mr Darling and Captain Hook in James Barrie's *Peter Pan*. Barrie was a close friend of the family and virtually adopted Daphne's cousins, the Llewelyn boys after the tragic deaths of their parents. The boys and their adventures with Barrie were the inspiration for *Peter Pan*.

She went to finishing school in Paris when she was 18. It was partly due to the unorthodox relationship that she struck up there with one of her French mistresses, Mlle Fernande Yvon, that the du Mauriers decided to buy Ferryside in Fowey by way of a distraction.

It was at Ferryside that she wrote *The Loving Spirit* (1931), followed in rapid succession by *I'll Never Be Young Again* (1932) and *Julius* (1933). Her future husband, Tommy 'Boy' Browning, inspired by his reading of her first novel sailed down to Fowey in his boat *Ygdrasil* to try to meet her.

He succeeded and they married in 1932. They would have three children, Tessa, Flavia and Christian (Kits).

In 1936, *Jamaica Inn* was published which really established her on the literary stage. In the same year she followed her husband to Alexandria in Egypt where he had been posted. She hated the social whirl of a commanding officer's wife – all 'cocktail parties and charades'. It was while she was here that, missing Cornwall desperately, she wrote her most famous novel *Rebecca*. Film rights, fame and fortune followed.

In 1940, she was back in England staying with the Puxley family at Langley End in Hertfordshire to be near to where her husband had been stationed. It was here that she wrote *Frenchman's Creek* (1941). She then lived briefly at Readymoney Cove in Fowey before managing to obtain a lease on the house she had coveted for so long, her 'House of Secrets', Menabilly.

The years at Menabilly would see the publication of *The King's General (1946)*, *My Cousin Rachel* (1951), the collection of short stories, *The Apple Tree* (1952), (which included *The Birds*) and *The Scapegoat* (1957).

In 1962, she completed an unfinished work by her great friend, Sir Arthur Quiller-Couch, *Castle Dor*. Her husband's health by this time was failing and he died in 1965. Shortly after, she learnt that the Rashleigh family did not intend to renew the lease on Menabilly. She would move to Kilmarth just along the headland.

Vanishing Cornwall (1967) was a non-fiction collaboration with her son, Kits Browning which served to heal the trauma she was going through. Inspired by the history of her new house and of the nearby town of Tywardreath and its former priory she wrote *The House on the Strand* in 1969.

Rule Britannia (1972) and an autobiography *Growing Pains* (1976), were her last major works before her death on 19 April, 1989. A memorial service followed at Tregaminion Church, near her Menabilly. Her ashes were scattered on the cliffs of the Gribbin Headland that she loved so well.

NOTES

1. Many have reported that incest – witness her frequent references to the Borgias – was a subject that fascinated du Maurier. Michael Thornton writes in an article in the *Daily Telegraph* that when he visits Menabilly with his sister the first question she fires at her young guests (her favourite torpedo as Thornton puts it) is: "You seem unusually close for brother and sister…tell me, what do you think both think about incest?" Thornton actually goes so far as to state that she had a terrible secret – that she began to encourage 'inappropriate intimacies' between her father and her herself. "We crossed the line" and I allowed it. He treated me like all the others- as if I was an actress playing his love interest in one of his plays"

2. The *Irene* has had, to put it mildly, a chequered career. Built in 1907, for 50 years she plied the coastal waters of Britain, transporting tiles, bricks, coal and clay. In 1965 she was found in a derelict state on the Hamble River by her present owner who spent 20 years restoring her to her former glory. As she was being sailed down the Thames to start her new life the bowsprit pierced the pavement of Hammersmith bridge, completely stopping the rush-hour traffic and cutting off the

gas supply to half of London! After a brief cinematic career (she played *The Flying Dutchman* in Richard Wagner's bio-film), she sailed to the Caribbean to join the charter business. There in 2003 fire started in the 'smokers' gallery' at the stern and she sank half-consumed by the flames. However, she rose yet again like a Phoenix – what we see today is in fact her third incarnation!

3 The *Janet Coombe*, in the early part of her career, because she was quick and manoeuvrable, specialised in the high-speed runs from the small ports of fruit-producing centres such as the Azores or the West Indies. Helen Doe's book shows that her first voyage took her from Palermo to New York laden with lemons and raisins.

4. Du Maurier's visit may have been prompted by Charles G. Harper's description of Millook in his 1910 *North Coast of Cornwall* guide. "People who really know how to make holiday come in two or three little parties and lie about in the sun, or bathe, or fish, or go boating, barelegged, in the oldest of old clothes, and not unfrequently in the scantiest of bathing dresses."

5. She had other memories she could bring to the scene as well. 1930 was a bad year for wrecks around Fowey. The yacht *Islander* broke up on rocks the night of 20 August in a terrific storm in Lantivet Bay. Coastguards saw people on board but were unable to save them. 4 lives were lost. Du Maurier recalls in her autobiography seeing the wreckage washed up over the following days.

6. In a wonderful example of the eccentricities of evolving etymology, Polridmouth (pronounced Pridmouth) shares in fact the same original meaning as Readymoney. Polridmouth was Porth Redeman in 1443. By 1613 it had become Pollradman. So by two separate processes of corruption, Redeman became Readymoney and Pollradman became Polridmouth, both meaning the cove of the ford of stones. And best of all, when they came to christen the stream running down to the beach here they called it – the Prid!

I owe this curious fact to *The River Fowey* by Wilson MacArthur – a charming book packed full of interesting information written by an author who was clearly enamoured of his partner endeavouring to feature her somewhere in the majority of the photos in the book, thus making it probably the earliest precursor (1948) to the *Where's Wally*? series.

7. One thing stands out: in most permutations, Mrs de Winter is Daphne du Maurier. Was she surprised, perhaps amused, that no-one really picked up on Max's comment at the beginning of the book? "I told you at the beginning of lunch you had a lovely and unusual name," he said. "I shall go further, if you will forgive me, and say that it becomes you as well as it became your father"

Even Hitchcock, apparently, on the set of *Rebecca* would refer to the character as Mrs Daphne de Winter.

8. Her mastery of her skill obviously takes time to develop. One of the less satisfactory aspects of her first major work *The Loving Spirit* is that, to a large extent, these two impulses have been 'compartmentalised'. Janet Coombe's 'masculine' aspirations and her, at times, quite subversive and uncomfortable relationship, dreamed or otherwise, with her son Joseph in the early part of the novel, give way completely at the close to the scenes of domestic bliss of Jennifer and her new husband. The 'happy ending' presumably reflects the fact that at this stage of her life she still saw marriage as a solution to her inner tensions. As she would learn, however, it is not through matrimony that the inner self is banished.

9. Much of the power of the short stories comes from this combination of bewildering beginnings which run headlong into disturbing endings without even the usual intermediary pause for breath that one has in the longer works.

10. Interestingly, the rhododendron was introduced into this country from Asia Minor 200 years ago – just about the time William Rashleigh was on his travels. There were practical as well as aesthetic reasons for its extensive planting on estates such as Menabilly: it provided exceptional cover for game.